The Complete
Stained Glass
Course

The Complete Stained Glass Course

HOW TO MASTER EVERY MAJOR GLASS WORK TECHNIQUE,
WITH THIRTEEN STUNNING PROJECTS TO CREATE

Lynette Wrigley and Marc Gerstein

APPLE

A QUINTET BOOK

Published by Apple Press
6 Blundell Street
London N7 9BH

First published in paperback in 2000
Reprinted 2001
ISBN 1-84092-274-5

This book was designed and produced by
Quintet Publishing Limited
6 Blundell Street
London N7 9BH

Creative Director: Richard Dewing
Designer: Ian Hunt/Linda Henley
Project Editor: Coral Walker
Photographer: Paul Forrester

Typeset in Great Britain by
Central Southern Typesetters, Eastbourne
Manufactured in Singapore by
Universal Graphics Pte Ltd
Printed in Singapore by
Star Standard Industries (Pte) Ltd

Contents

❖ ❖ ❖

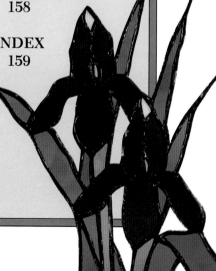

Introduction

 Our book is by no means a complete guide to all the processes and techniques of decorative glasswork that has developed over the centuries. That would require several volumes, each devoted to a particular aspect of decorative glass. What we have done is to focus on the main skills and offer readers the opportunity to learn a basic, working knowledge of each technique. With our teaching experience and your skills, the simple instructions and photography will enhance and increase your desire to explore the possibilities of the craft. By supplying a basic framework, it is our hope that the creativity in you will flourish and discover a means of expression.

WHAT IS STAINED GLASS?

Stained glass is actually an accepted misnomer of words to describe all colored and painted glass used in a decorative way. In reality there are two distinct types of "stained glass" that bear a resemblance to one another but, in fact, are quite different. The delicate figures seen in church windows are really quite separate from the Tiffany glass lampshades found in bars, restaurants and private homes. In reality, any work that relies solely on the innate qualities of colored glass could more accurately be described as "glass art". Stained glass should only refer to colored or plain glass that has been painted, decorated or further processed by the artist themselves. However, the term itself is now so widely accepted that "stained glass" is understood to encompass everything from a simple colored glass window ornament to a magnificently stained and painted church window.

A SHORT HISTORY

The likely origins of glass are believed to emanate from the Egyptians, where glass was possibly first used as jewelry. From Egypt the use of glass radiated outwards to Byzantium and then to Greece and Rome. It is known from the excavations of Herculaneum and Pompeii that the Romans were the first to use glass as a window by placing pieces in the openings of their stonework. The craft developed and in time glass blowing replaced moulding. Technical skills improved and glass became transparent as opposed to translucent. The influence of the glass worker eventually found its way to France where stained glass windows as we know them today first developed. Throughout the Middle Ages, stained glass was an ecclesiastical art form which helped to educate a largely illiterate population in the stories of the Bible. It is possible that the earliest known stained glass windows are those in the Augesburg Cathedral in Germany and date from the 11th century. The famous windows of Chartres in France and Canterbury and York in England to name but a few came later.

RIGHT *A glorious example of leaded work using fragments of hand-painted Victorian glass which the artist collected during a period as a glass restorer.*

LEO AMERY

The high point for these medieval windows was around the 13th and 14th centuries.

In the 16th century came the rebellion against Rome and commissioned religious work declined dramatically. By Royal decree many pieces of fine glass were systematically destroyed as stained glass was considered too ornate and extravagant for the protestant church of the time. Not only was this disastrous for the existing stained glass craft but there was yet more trouble for the manufacturers on the European continent who had developed the technique of making colored glass into a highly specialized industry. Many of the glass houses or producers situated in the Lorraine were destroyed by war in 1633 and the secrets and techniques of glass making lay buried in the rubble for centuries to come.

The craft now directed itself towards heraldic and domestic windows and there became a period when clear or white glass as it is now known was painted with enamels.

In place of the richly colored medieval windows which had transmitted light, the new work seemed dull and opaque in comparison.

Fortunately the 19th century witnessed a revival and the beauty of stained glass was rediscovered. In 1850 the formula for making medieval colored glass was re-formulated and in the 1860s William Morris revived the medieval expertise by using this new style of colored glass in his windows. Edward Burne Jones also contributed considerably to popularizing stained glass and these men – among others – designed windows not only for churches but also for domestic settings. Stained glass was once again thriving.

In America, there was also an enormous influence on glass by Louis Comfort Tiffany, who broke away from the traditions of joining glass with lead channels by inventing the copper foil technique. Tiffany, the son of the famous jeweler, also experimented with the design and fabrication of glass and developed opalescent glass which he used for his prolific production of lampshades.

In the last twenty years there has been a tremendous interest in stained glass as a growing hobby and craft industry. Old window panels are carefully restored to their former glory and new works are commissioned to reflect the architecture of today. Stained glass is seen as both a craft that can be learned as a satisfying hobby and an independent art form. Many recently commissioned works can now be seen in public buildings, museums, bars and restaurants. No longer is it considered or perceived as an exclusively ecclesiastical art. Modern styles using bold, colorful themes are found within buildings constructed within the last 50 years. Post-war Germany, in particular, has a tradition of incorporating decorative art into every public building. Many impressive modern windows have been commissioned and the work of Schaffrath has set a standard and influence on many glass students.

For those interested in taking up glass as a hobby, there is an ever increasing wealth of new materials, information and equipment available. Stained glass instruction is frequently offered and it is now possible to learn the most basic techniques in weekend or evening courses. Our book has taken advantage of the current revival of decorative glasswork and offers a combination of information, techniques and projects to inspire you to explore further.

CHAPTER ONE

Glass

❖ ❖ ❖

 It's hard to imagine a world without the plain, featureless material known as glass. From fiber optics used in communications to an everyday wine bottle, glass is a material that has woven itself into every corner of our daily lives. Aside from new, efficient manufacturing processes, the actual makeup of glass has remained basically unchanged from the first crude vessel cast in the ancient world.

Today, there is a vast range of colored and clear glass from which to choose, both hand- and machine-made. This chapter will take you through the different types of glass to help you in your selection. The principal ingredients of all types of glass are silica sand, soda ash and limestone. The soda ash acts as a flux facilitating the melting of the sand, while the limestone is added as a stabilizer, making the finished product more durable. Colors in glass are created by blending natural metallic oxides into the raw materials. Cadmium sulphide creates yellow, cobalt creates blue, while true pinks can only be made with gold.

Glass manufacturing has been – and still is – very much a process of experimenting, adjusting and personalizing the basic recipe to achieve a variety of results. Glass artists today benefit from a huge range of glass supplied by different manufacturers each offering their own individual and identifiable product.

Buying glass for your projects is a stimulating process; it's satisfying assessing the many colors and textures while trying to visualize how they can be worked into your design.

Glass is divided into two general types: antique or mouth-blown glass and machine-made glass. Within these two groups are many sub-groups of specialized glass.

WHICH GLASS TO CHOOSE?

"How well does it cut?" is very often the first question we are asked and unfortunately there is no firm answer. After glass has been formed into sheets it is slowly heated and then cooled. This process – called annealing – removes the stress or tension within the sheet making it possible to cut. Glass that hasn't been well annealed is termed "fiery", often breaking erratically when scored with the cutter. Antique glass occasionally has this tendency, more so when making the first cut on a full stock sheet. Hot colors like red and yellow can also be slightly more difficult to cut as the glass itself has a harder surface.

Antique Glass

Red flashed glass reveals a traditional floral pattern.

 Favored by glass artists, each sheet of antique glass is blown into a cylinder or "muff", which is annealed, cut down the length with a glass cutter, and reheated to be flattened into a sheet. The individual skills and years of experience required to become a proficient glass maker necessitate that "antiqued" glass is more expensive than machine-made glass. The uneven texture, brilliant surface qualities and array of "imperfections" give each sheet a distinctive character.

PLAIN ANTIQUE: Only one color.

STREAKY ANTIQUE: Two or more colors swirled together making sheets of this glass appear like a delicate watercolor painting locked within each sheet.

CLEAR REAMY: Available in clear or tint colors. Each sheet is characterized by great surface movement giving the glass a "windy" effect.

SEEDY AND CLEAR: Light tints or clear glass that has been purposely made with the air bubbles to distort and refract light.

CRACKLE: Antique glass that is rapidly cooled to distress the surface.

FLASHED: A thin layer or flash of glass laid on a base color or clear glass. The thin flash can then be etched or sandblasted away exposing the contrasting base color.

A starburst design on brilliant blue flashed glass.

Glass Types

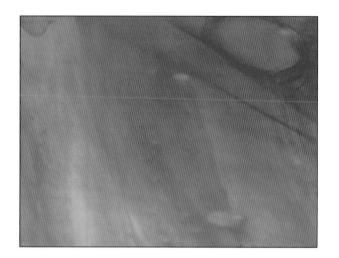

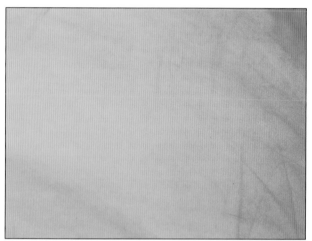

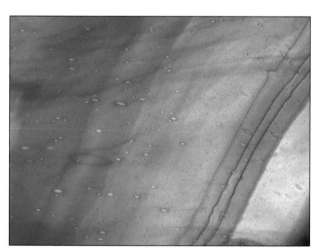

It's tremendously exciting to see the enormous range of colored glass now available. These examples of streaky antique glass demonstrate the wonderful array of colors and patterns you can buy for your projects.

Glass Types

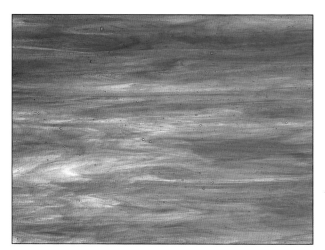

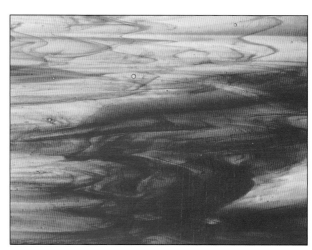

ABOVE *Four examples of streaky cathedral glass.*

LEFT *The machine-made Spectrum baroque.*

Semi-antique Glass

 Midway between blown antique and machine-rolled glass is semi-antique. Often called drawn antique, this type of glass is pulled or drawn from the molten furnace and allowed to anneal and harden in air giving it a smooth and brilliant surface on both sides. Available in many color tints, with either a plain or wavy surface, semi-antique is considerably less expensive than the handmade variety.

Machine-rolled Glass

Nowhere has the interest in art glass become more apparent than in the manufacture of rolled color glass. Glass manufacturers both in the United States and Europe offer hundreds of colors, patterns and densities. As the name implies, the molten glass is rolled out by machine on a flat surface. Various textures and patterns can be impressed on the semi-fluid glass surface as it is passed through rollers. Like antique glass, the various rolled glass manufacturers each have their own particular style of creating glass which is easily identifiable. Because of its lower cost, availability and diversity, rolled glass is the most frequently used glass for newcomers.

The actual production of rolled glass is an exciting feast of color, heat and motion. Glass manufacturers, Spectrum have combined modern technology with old world methods to produce an extensive range of quality machine glass.

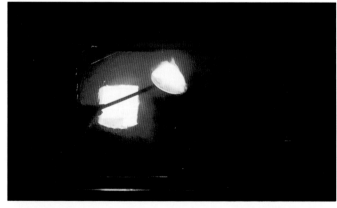

The primary glass furnace with 30 tons of hot glass. To this is added the particular color being produced. This method of production known as "continuous ribbon" is unique to Spectrum.

Glass Types

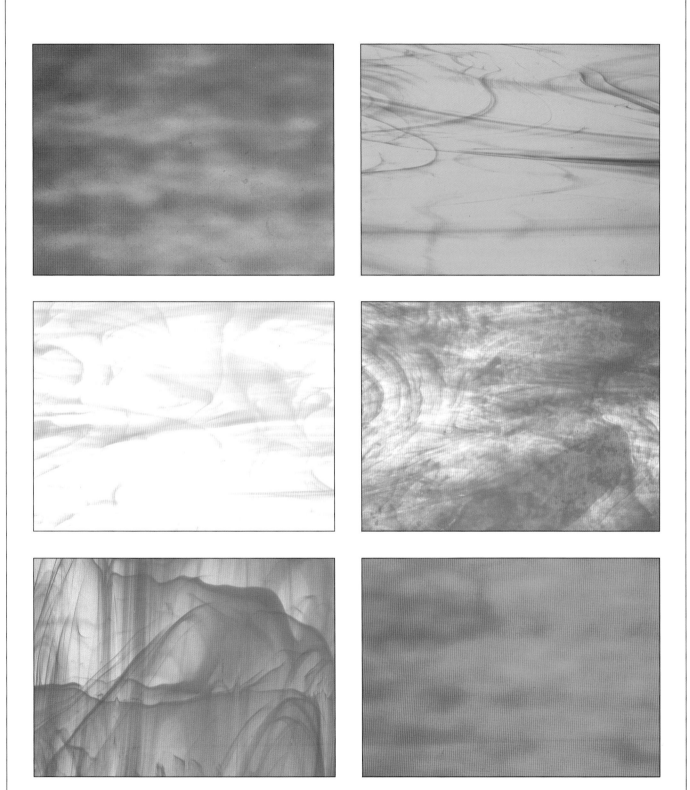

*Less expensive than hand fabricated glass, machine
rolled glass is nevertheless produced in a
wide range of types, styles and colors.*

Hand-rolled Glass

Each piece of specialty art glass is individually hand rolled creating details, colors and textures that could never be duplicated by machine. Glass similar to the innovative work of Tiffany continues to be produced by small specialty companies concentrating on this beautiful and unusual glass.

FRACTURE AND STREAMER GLASS

The production of fracture and streamer glass by the Uroboros Glass Company. First a large bubble is blown then broken: that creates the fractures. The molten fractures and streamers are spread by hand as the sheet is rolled out.

Glass Types

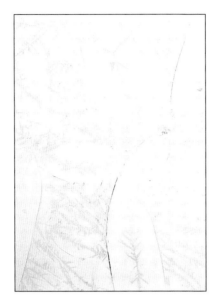

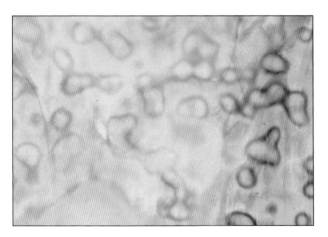
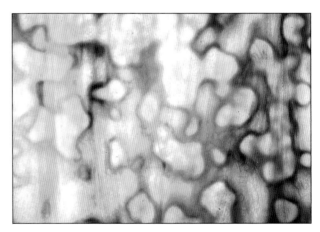
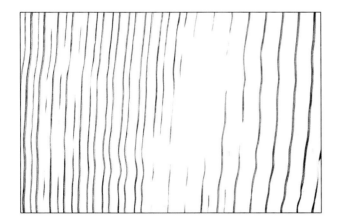
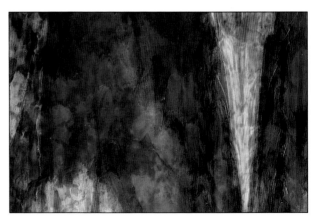

*A selection of hand-rolled glass: no two
sheets will be identical.*

Roundels and nuggets

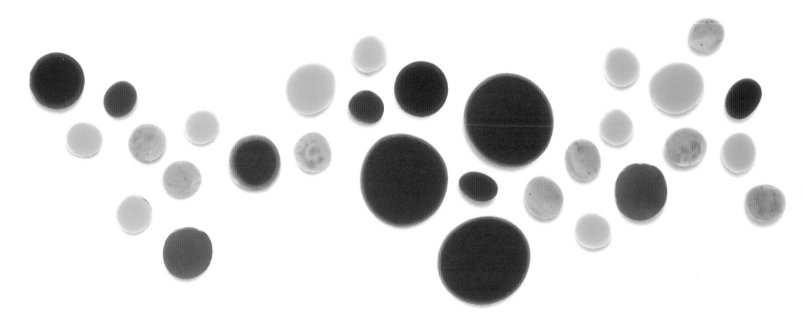

 Roundels and nuggets are wonderfully tactile small pieces of glass used for various decorative purposes. Nuggets, for example, are often used in projects other than stained glass work; jewelry being one. Roundels are beautiful pieces of glass which the manufacturer makes by spinning molten glass into small circles. These are available in a wide range of colors for use in Victorian-style leaded lights.

CUT GLASS GEMS

Cut glass gems are rather like nuggets, but instead they are made with many facets and highly polished to reflect the light. Gems radiate color and, in some cases, will refract light.

Glass Types

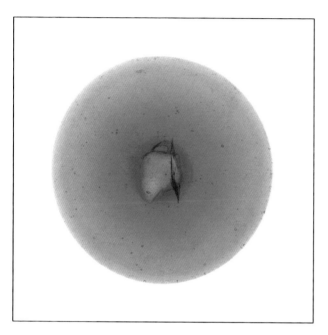

Circles of colored glass with smooth edges come in various sizes. They are either hand spun or pressed by machine and used most frequently in leaded lights.

Cut glass gems

Glass Types

Examples of plain antique glass.

Glass Types

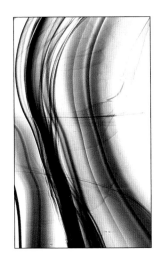

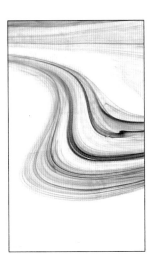

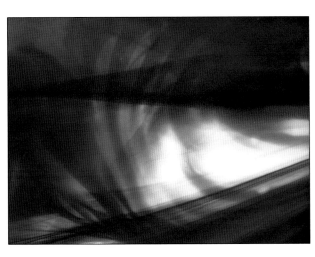
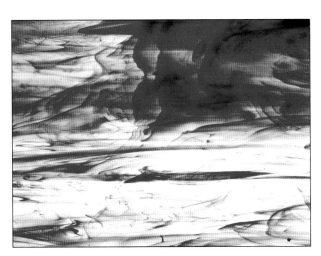

Examples of Baroque glass; the two pieces on the right are iridized.

Glass Types

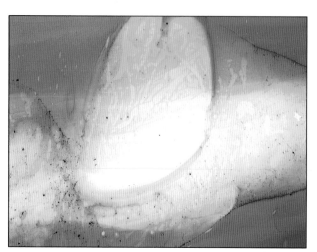

ABOVE: *Two wonderful pieces of antique streaky. The piece on the left is a beautiful example of pink-gold.*
BELOW: *Plain antique glass.*

CHAPTER TWO

How to work with glass

❖ ❖ ❖

Not surprisingly, many beginners are nervous when handling glass, frightened it might break easily and that they could injure themselves. Although glass is fragile, it is also remarkably robust. How you handle it is often the key to success. This chapter focuses on the basic skills of glass cutting: the tools you will need and the techniques to develop. Once you gain confidence, cutting and handling glass will, like most skills, become second nature.

Like any other craft or trade, stained glass has its own specialized range of tools and materials. The tools of the trade are, in fact, perfect examples of logic and simplicity. Glasswork is very much a hands-on craft and the tools have evolved to fit the hand comfortably for a specific function. Much of the equipment that has been introduced in the last 20 years is in response to the growing demand from hobbyists for easier and more convenient tools. With relatively little outlay, an individual can purchase a basic set of tools enabling him or her to create intricate, professional results – remember, the skill is in the hand not the tool!

Because stained glass is a specialized craft, we recommend the best place to start looking for information is with a specialist company. A general tool merchant or glass shop is generally not able to advise or supply you so well. There are many small glass studios that both create their own work and offer a supply service. Look in the telephone book under "Stained Glass" and find out if they have a genuine interest in the supply of tools and information. A good supplier will be invaluable, not only for the basics but also for advice on techniques and materials as your work progresses. Very often, a catalog will be available providing both a mail order service and a helpful description of products.

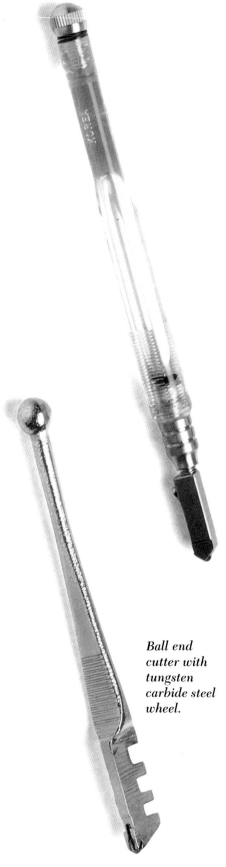

Ball end cutter with tungsten carbide steel wheel.

Cutting Equipment

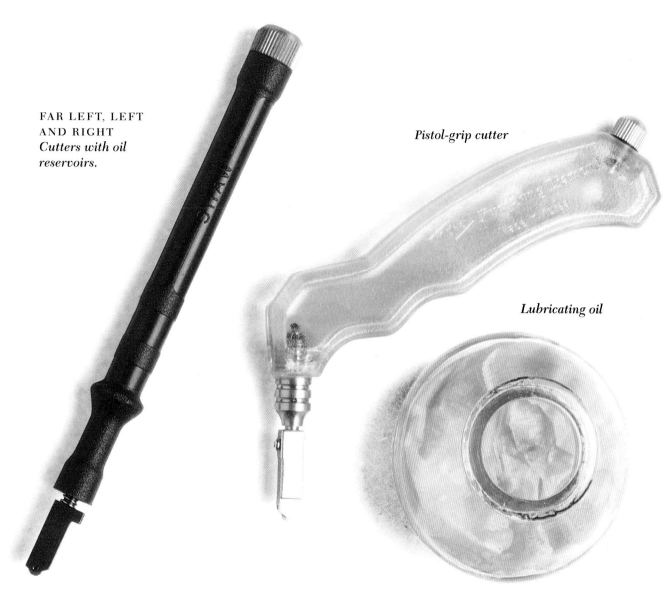

FAR LEFT, LEFT
AND RIGHT
*Cutters with oil
reservoirs.*

Pistol-grip cutter

Lubricating oil

GLASS CUTTERS

A glass cutter is not actually a cutter in the traditional sense like a hack saw or scissors. In fact, glass isn't really cut in any way that resembles the cutting of wood, metal or cloth. The glass cutter offers a much more subtle method of changing large pieces of glass into smaller, intricate shapes. All glass cutters have a hard steel wheel that will scratch or score the glass surface. We always recommend that you purchase the best cutter you can afford as this tool is really the key to working with glass. Although the quality of the cutters will vary from a cheap plastic handle cutter through a sophisticated charmer with a brass handle and oil reservoir it is really the skill and technique of the individual that is most important. To date, there are literally dozens of different cutters on the market made to fit the hand comfortably. Like feet, hands are quite particular to the individual and it's best to "try on" several styles to discover the one that feels right before making a purchase. When considering different types of glass cutter don't choose a multiple wheel cutter. These are generally of a poor quality and even worse, the large head will hide the cut line from view, which is in effect like driving with a blindfold. Diamond cutters, tricky to use, are only suitable for straight lines and should not be considered for use in stained glass.

The most important part of any cutter is the cutting wheel. The quality of the wheel will influence how well and how long the cutter will last. We can divide glass cutters into three general groups by the type of wheel.

STEEL WHEEL CUTTER: The classic pencil grip cutter with or without a ball end has been cutting glass since the mid 1800s. Most people will be introduced to cutting with this tool and although it looks painfully simple when compared to newer shapes, it is a precise and capable tool. The three grooves or indentations on this cutter were at one time covered with a soft metal and used to shape glass. The soft metal insertions are no longer available, making the grooves on the classic cutter about as useful as tailfins on a car. The steel wheel cutter is a good introductory tool, but it will soon wear out.

CARBIDE STEEL CUTTERS: Although identical in appearance to steel, these offer at least five times more life and require less pressure, making them easier to use. When making the transition from steel to carbide steel most people will initially apply excessive pressure and score the glass too deeply. The ball end cutter illustrated is available with a replaceable carbide wheel and is the favored tool of many older glass cutters who learned on this venerable classic. It has a cast iron handle, a weighty feel and is a pleasure to use.

TUNGSTEN CARBIDE STEEL: The third general type of cutters were introduced to the market relatively recently and if the term "revolutionize glass cutting" can be applied, these cutters would get the credit. The cutting wheel is upgraded to tungsten carbide steel and is much smaller in diameter than the conventional carbide or steel wheel. Smaller, harder wheels translate into less pressure and are therefore easier to control when scoring. Like turning on a bike with small tires, these cutters are excellent for intricate pieces with the tight curves favored by many glass workers today.

Designers of these cutters have also applied the science of ergonomics by creating handles that fit the hand with a natural, easy grip. These tools, known as the super cutters, have introduced glass cutting to many people who never felt at ease with the pencil shape of the classic. Most will contain an oil reservoir which constantly lubricates the cutting wheel when scoring. Some can be gripped like a tennis racket, others have thick handles large enough to accommodate two hands when cutting.

Glass cutters, like toothbrushes, are very personal items and shouldn't be loaned or borrowed. If properly cared for they can give years of good service, however, the cutting wheel will eventually wear out and need to be replaced. There are companies that will re-sharpen dull cutting wheels but usually the expense and time involved makes replacement a better alternative.

ABOVE *Lubricate your cutter from time to time with light machine oil or mineral spirit so that the wheel turns freely. Keep a small jar by your work area and keep a pad of cotton soaked in oil. Lubricating the wheel will prolong its life and improve the score. Some cutters are self-lubricating (see page 25).*

Snippers

GLASS PLIERS

Second only to the glass cutter, glass pliers are the tool you will become most familiar with when working glass. Pliers are used for shaping and breaking glass after it has been scored with the cutter. Although similar in appearance to a pair of general household pliers, glass pliers are very specialized and are easily damaged if used for repairing your bicycle, or mending your fence. In our studio work we have found that there are three types of plier used in our day-to-day work. Pliers made for the glazing trade tend to be heavy handed tools for working with plate glass and are seldom used with colored glasswork.

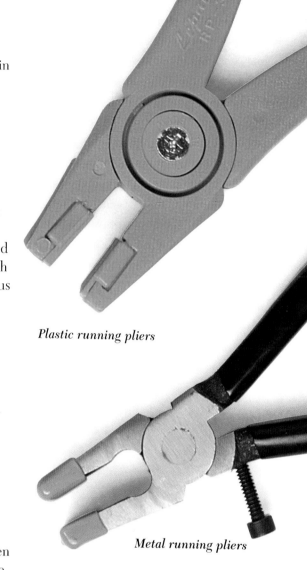

GROZING PLIERS: The grozing pliers are by far the most important pliers in your tool box and are in constant use for a great many tasks. Made from a soft metal, the lower jaw of the pliers is curved and serrated to grip and hold the glass effectively. Most groziers are now supplied with a spring-loaded handle that returns to the open position when in use, thus reducing fatigue. The primary use of the grozier is to nibble and shape irregular pieces glass; its narrow jaw width make the grozier particularly suitable for reaching inside curves.

Plastic running pliers

BREAKING PLIERS: Our breaking pliers tend to get the most use when someone has either borrowed or misplaced the grozier. Usually slightly heavier than a grozier, with wider jaws, the breakers are used for breaking off straight line scores on larger sections of glass.

RUNNING PLIERS: Long, straight and narrow pieces of glass will often break in two (or three) when separated from a larger sheet. The running pliers are constructed solely for the purpose of successfully separating these thin, sometimes difficult straight cuts. The inside of the jaws are either curved or have a raised center section which is lined up directly over a cut. When pressure is applied to the score it will very often run with a satisfying click, neatly separating a thin strip of glass. Available in plastic or metal, the running pliers are a useful tool for their very specific task.

Metal running pliers

Grozer breakers

Grinding

ELECTRIC GLASS GRINDER

When running beginners' workshops, this machine is well hidden under the table. So strong is the allure of the grinder that, given the chance, many of our students would learn glass grinding rather than glass cutting. Glass pushed against the water cooled, diamond impregnated, spinning wheel becomes perfectly smooth with minimal effort. The shape of a piece of glass can be changed in seconds. Beginners will often rely too much on the machine rather than perfecting their skills of accurate cutting. Once confident with a cutter and pliers, however, the grinder becomes a valuable, labor-saving machine that encourages people to move on to more ambitious projects.

Various bit sizes and grits can be installed which will either aggressively remove an area of glass or leave an almost polished edge. Care must be taken to keep the water coolant level high and always to wear eye protection if the machine is not fitted with an eye shield.

Electric grinding machine and safety goggles.

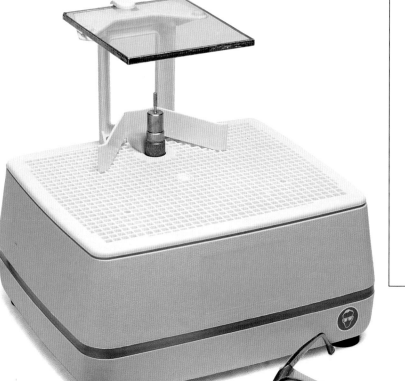

CARBORUNDUM OR WET STONE

As many of us painfully know, glass frequently breaks with a razor sharp edge. The carborundum stone dulls the edges, making them safe to handle. Although time consuming, compared with the electric grinding machine, the carborundum stone is inexpensive and effective. You can wet the stone to minimize glass dust and to use simply rub the edges of the glass along the sides of the stone.

Glass Cutting Aids

 Most glass cutting is freehand, so it's just you, your cutter and the glass. Stained glass windows for the most part are one-off designs that usually do not require a great many repetitive, identical shapes. However, cutting aids exist which make short, accurate work of tasks that could otherwise take hours by freehand with less than perfect results.

THE CUTTING SQUARE

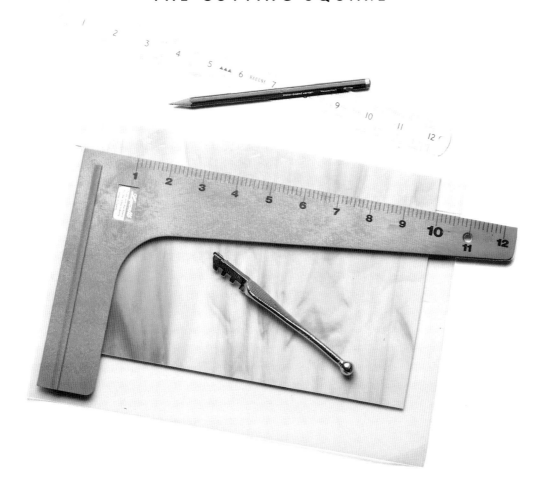

No matter how steady your hand, the only way to cut a perfectly straight line is to use a cutting edge or square. The squares that are used for glass cutting have a 90 degree runner or stop along the lower edge which both prevents the edge from moving and gives a perfect square cut.

This is especially useful for squaring off sheets when it is necessary to work from a straight line. Squares are available in many lengths and most studios will require a long one – at least one yard – for cutting down stock sheets and several smaller ones for squaring up individual pieces.

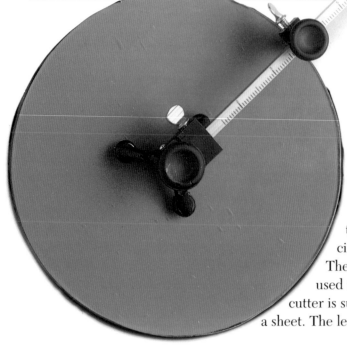

THE CIRCLE/STRIP CUTTER

Learning to cut a circle freehand is an important skill which encompasses many vital cutting steps. However, like a straight line, a perfectly round circle can only be cut with a specific circle cutter. Circles are not a frequent shape in glass design but the circle cutter has a certain novelty value that some people will find hard to resist. A turret with either a suction cup or rubber tip legs is held firmly on the glass surface. A metal rod with an adjustable cutting head rotates around the axis of this turret scoring the glass. Beam cutters of this type will cut circles as small as 3 inches in diameter.

The strip cutter is usually supplied with the circle cutter and is used to cut long straight strips. The turret used on the circle cutter is substituted for a guide that follows along the straight edge of a sheet. The length of strip is simply determined by the size of the sheet.

IRREGULAR SHAPE CUTTER

Few glass artists would require this type of machine for bulk cutting or repetitious shapes (see below). Shape cutters are generally used in production studios where quantities of perfect repeats are required for lampshades or light-catchers. A glass cutting wheel, mounted on a stylus is guided around a template making an identical score on each piece of glass. The pressure of the score on the glass is regulated by compressed air, making these machines incredibly fast and simple to use.

The rubber-tipped feet grip the center of the glass and the cutting head is positioned on the guideline.

Once the glass has been scored, tangent scores must be made so the circle can be broken easily.

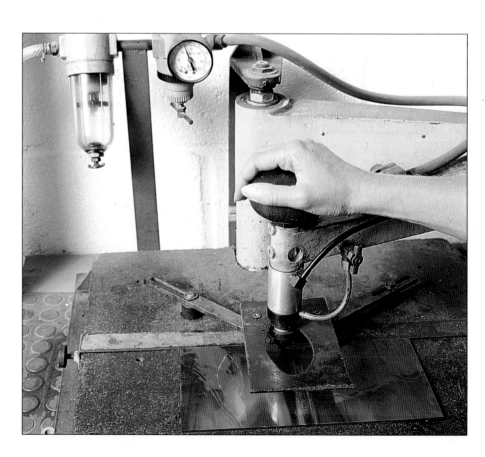

Glass Cutting

Cutting glass is not as difficult as many people imagine. By following some simple but essential guidelines you will soon develop confidence in your glass cutting abilities. Persevere and practise on clear scrap glass. There are several recommended ways of holding a cutter but there are now several types of cutter on the market and styles of holding the cutter for comfort and efficiency will vary. We have emphasized our favored style because we have found in our experience of teaching it works best. However individual preference will develop and providing the chosen method produces the desired result without unnecessary effort – there's no reason why you shouldn't use it.

Ask a glass merchant to let you have some offcuts of thin clear window glass, which is easy to work with and cheap for practising.

HOLDING THE CUTTER

 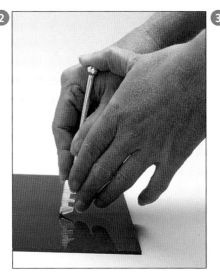 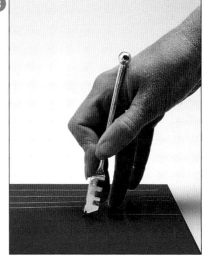

1 Try to hold the glass cutter in different ways until you find one which suits you. One method is to hold the cutter as if it were a pencil. Hold the cutter firmly using the thumb and index finger to grip the handle and allow the shank to rest against the hand.

2 Sometimes it helps to use the other hand for extra pressure. Place the thumb of the other hand on the end of the cutter and stretch the fingers down to rest pressure next to the cutting head.

3 Place the cutter on the glass at about an angle of just below 90 degrees. Practise scoring by placing the cutting wheel at the near edge of the glass and press the cutter down while pushing slowly and steadily to the other edge of the glass. You should bear down with enough pressure to be able to hear the wheel scoring the surface. Keep the pressure and the speed constant. The score will appear as a fracture on the glass.

WORK SURFACE

A hard wood or similar table top will cause the glass to slide around and become scratched, so it must be covered. We have used cardboard, cork, heavy craft paper, a thin pile or carpet underlay with good results. Keep a pan and brush handy and frequently brush off the tiny shards of glass that will be produced on every cut. You are more likely to obtain small cuts with these tiny needles of glass when you inadvertently brush them off the table with your hand than at any other time. Use a brush!

IMPORTANT HINTS

❖ Always stand when cutting glass and work on a flat and steady work surface.

❖ Make sure your table is not too high – just below waist level is a fair measure.

❖ Never go over the score line twice. If the score you made was not successful, start a new score in a different place on the glass. Going over the old score again will just create a dull gouge in the glass and in time will ruin the cutting wheel.

❖ If the glass is textured always score on the smooth side.

❖ If you do not hear the sound of scoring on the glass then it is more than likely that you are not using enough pressure.

❖ Do not lift the cutter off the glass until the score is complete.

❖ Always make sure that a score travels from one edge of the glass to another. You cannot start or stop in the middle of a piece of glass.

❖ Keep a dustpan and brush next to you and remember to make a habit of brushing up the shards of glass as you work.

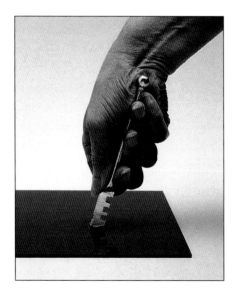

Make sure that you hold the cutter comfortably. Adjust your fingers and thumb and the angle of the cutter until you feel relaxed.

Experiment by adjusting the positions of your finger and thumb slightly and by changing the angle at which you hold the cutter to give a better score. If your score is too faint, apply more pressure until you can both see and hear the cut line appear. How you feel most comfortable holding the cutter will vary according to the style of cutter. How well you have scored the glass will become evident when you begin to break the score apart. Scored glass should always be broken or snapped while the score is still new.

To break the piece of glass apart once it has been scored, you can use one of several methods shown opposite and overleaf.

HANDS

Achieving a clean break is one of the most satisfying aspects of cutting, and you will feel a great sense of achievement when you break a score using just your hands.

Hold the scored piece firmly, with a thumb on each side of the score line and with your index fingers underneath and either side of the score; snap the glass by moving your wrists sharply outwards. Always keep your thumbs and fingers next to the score and grip the glass firmly while snapping apart.

GLASS PLIERS

Pliers are especially useful when you want to break off a piece of glass that is too small or very narrow or just awkward to be broken by hand. Place the tip of the pliers next to the score line. Hold the glass tightly in one hand and grip the glass well with the pliers in the other. While gripping the glass with the pliers, pull and snap apart.

Glass pliers are also used to break off any small irregular edges on a straight or curved score.

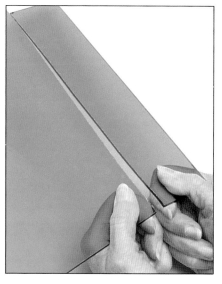

ABOVE *To snap apart a piece by hand, place the thumbs on top and curl the fingers underneath and either side of the score. Make a sharp outward movement of the wrist while gripping the glass between the fingers and thumbs.*

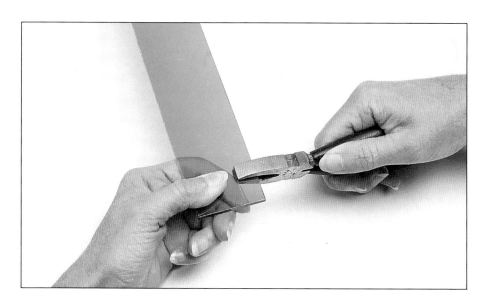

LEFT *If the strip of glass you want is too narrow for your fingers, use the pliers. Put the edge of the pliers in line with the score and grip the glass. Keep the fingers and thumbs of the other hand close to the score and hold the glass steady.*

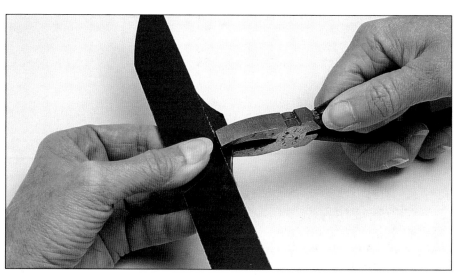

LEFT *Glass does not always break just as you would like. Trim the score with the pliers. Always place the pliers next to the score and with a firm and confident grip, snap off the unwanted glass.*

TAPPING

Tapping is particularly useful and often necessary for breaking curved scores and is the most reliable method of encouraging a score to break on difficult glass. If you feel you have made a good score but are unable to break the glass apart with your hands or the pliers, tapping will usually always help you out. As you tap you will see the appearance of the score change as a fracture develops.

To break the glass, hold the cutter with your fingers and thumb and tap directly on the score line from underneath with the ball end of the cutter. As you tap, the appearance of the line should begin to change. If it does not, tap a little harder, still taking care to strike the glass directly under the score line. Hold the piece of glass very firmly while you tap, supporting it in preparation for pieces falling on the table. When tapping remember that you need only give a controlled but very firm "tap" under the score. There is no need to swing the ball cutter wildly.

Tap the score with the ball end of the cutter.

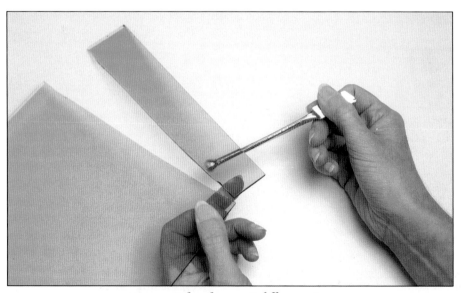

Support the glass as it falls apart.

BENCH METHOD

You can break a larger piece of glass in two by placing the scored lines on the edge of a table, then raise the glass and bring it back down again sharply. The downward force will cause the score to break on the edge of the table. This procedure can only be used for straight cuts. Don't use this method on anything larger than 1 square foot of glass.

After you have scored and broken some pieces of glass you will notice there may be tiny protrusions and sometimes narrow slices of glass on the edges of the glass. These can be taken off using the same pliers you used for breaking. This is called grozing. By holding the glass gently between the jaws of the pliers and rolling the pliers up or down you will be able to remove these small slivers. A tiny chip on the edge of the glass that refuses to shift can be all that prevents your piece of glass from fitting perfectly. Take it off by squeezing the chip with the tip of the pliers and literally nipping it away with a sharp downward movement of the pliers.

Use the edge of the table to help break the glass.

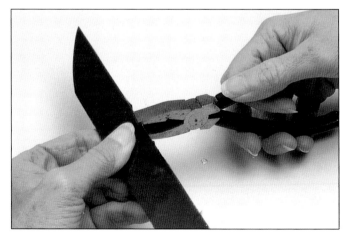

Untidy edges can be grozed off. Close the pliers over the glass. Maintain a loose hold and rotate them gently up or down. The "teeth" inside the mouth of the pliers will groze away these edges.

Small jagged bits of glass can be "nipped" away. Use just the tip of the pliers to hold the glass, squeeze them and nip off the tiny pieces.

CUTTING A WAVY LINE

After practising scoring and breaking random lines across some scrap glass, try some wavy lines or actual shapes. Practise breaking with your hands and also the pliers. Right angles cannot be cut from glass and to cut certain shapes there are particular rules to follow.

1 Simple curved shapes can usually be broken with pliers but occasionally – depending on the type of glass – there may be some resistance. A few short, sharp taps with the ball end of the cutter can help to release the tension in the score. As you tap, you will see the score change in appearance.

2 Support the glass while you tap.

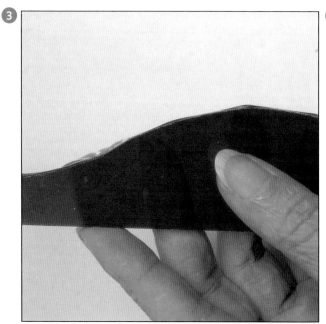

3 Once the curve has been tapped it will probably still show jagged edges. These must be grozed away.

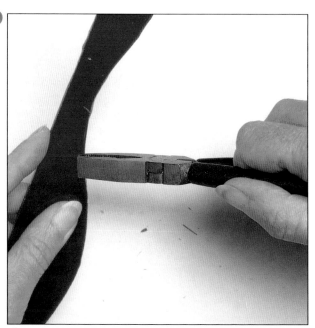

4 Groze the edges using the pliers. Hold the pliers gently, don't grip too tightly, and rotate them. The "teeth" of the pliers will remove these pieces.

CUTTING ANGLES

You cannot simply cut a right or acute angle from a piece of glass. Instead, you must plan your scores carefully to enable you to achieve the desired result. Below, we show how to cut a right angle and a "v" shape in glass.

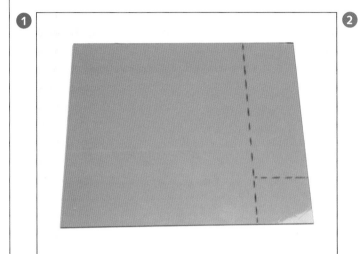

1 The dotted lines indicate the necessary direction of the scores: the first one being the vertical.

2 The first score is broken.

3 The second score is broken.

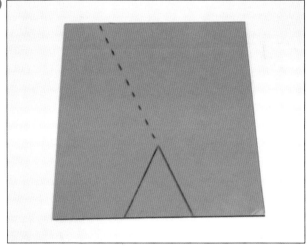

4 The "v" could not be cut out of a piece of glass by hand unless you follow the dotted lines which indicate the first score.

CUTTING A CIRCLE

True circles must be scored first with a circle cutter, see page 00. Once this is done, you will need to make many tangent scores off the circle for the glass to break correctly.

1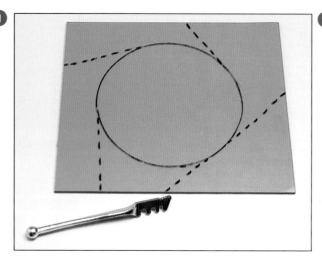

1 The dotted lines represent the suggested direction and angle of the scores. Start from one edge of the glass and move the score to meet the circle. Travel some way around the circle and then move the score away to another edge.

2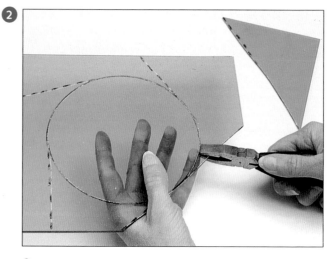

2 Place the pliers next to the score and break off the first pieces..

3

3 Move around the circle and continue to break off each section.

4

4 Use the pliers to "nip" off the sharp points. Grip the point with the tip of the pliers.

CUTTING A CURVE

Cutting a convex curve will require more than one score.

Make the first score following the line of the curve required. With great care make more scores within the curve. Make as many as you can close together. These inner scores can be tapped gently to loosen the tension and then break out these series of inner scores, with the pliers, removing them one at a time. Be cautious as you get further into the series of curves and if the scores still seem tight when you apply the pliers then resort to a little tapping to loosen them.

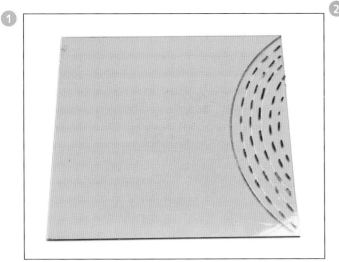

1 The dotted lines represent the suggested score lines. Make a succession of scores inside the initial one. The deeper the curve the more you may need to make.

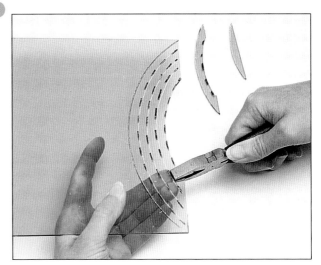

2 Keep a steady hold of the glass with one hand. Use the pliers to gently but firmly "pull" out the scored sections.

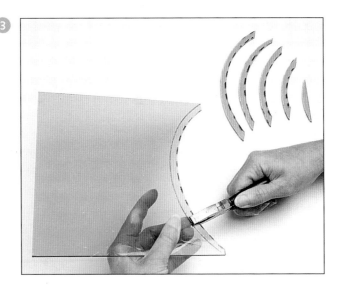

3 As you become familiar with different glass, you will learn when it is best to use pliers or when tapping will be advantageous.

USING A STRAIGHT EDGE

In our experience of teaching we find using a straight edge is a method that requires some practice. It is also probably the only time that you will need to pull the cutter towards the body instead of away from you.

The trick of using a straight edge is to remember to put enough pressure on the ruler to hold it steady while you are also putting pressure on the cutter while drawing it towards you and against the side of the ruler. The most common problem you will encounter is that the ruler will slip. A straight edge with a rubber backing will cling to the glass firmly and prevent it from moving while scoring.

TRANSPARENT GLASS

When cutting transparent glass, place the design or pattern on the work surface and the glass over the top. You can then cut directly on to the glass following visible lines of the pattern underneath.

OPALESCENT GLASS

As opalescent glass is not transparent you would normally use a light box. The pattern would be placed between the light box and the piece of glass. As opal glass does transmit artificial light you will be able to see the pattern and can cut directly on to the glass following the lines underneath.

When cutting dense opal glass, use carbon paper to put the cut lines directly on the glass surface. Place a piece of carbon paper between the glass and the pattern. Using a fine pen or pencil, trace over the cut line on the pattern transferring the image on to the glass. Now cut directly on to the glass following the carbon line.

Transparent glass can be simply laid over the pattern ready for scoring.

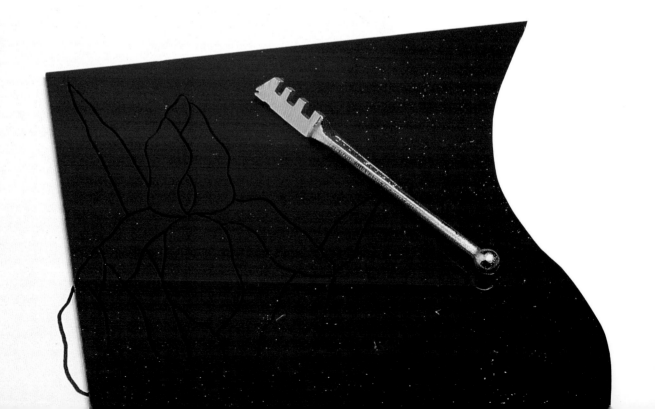

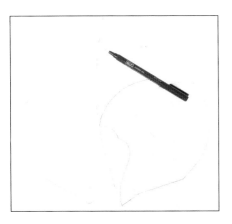

Templates are necessary for opalescent glass. They are cut-outs of the pattern which you can draw around directly on to the glass.

MIRRORED GLASS

Always cut mirrored glass on the reflective side. Protect the backing which is sensitive to scratching by brushing away any tiny glass shards on the work surface.

TEMPLATES

With opalescent glass or any glass that is not easy to see through you can also make templates if you don't have a light box handy. Templates are simply cut-out patterns of your design.

Place a piece of paper over your design and trace it. Cut out the shapes accurately and lay them back on the design to check that they fit. Place these templates on to the glass and draw around them with a felt tip pen or glass crayon. Now cut these shapes following the lines.

SAFETY

❖ Always wear safety glasses when cutting glass.

❖ Tiny particles of glass will flake off your cutting lines. These should be swept away regularly. Although it may be tempting to use the side of your hand, don't – this simple action is the cause of most minor cuts.

❖ Keep only the pieces of glass you are using on the work surface. Do not allow discarded pieces and offcuts to accumulate in a pile. Discard or store them safely.

❖ Handle pieces of glass firmly and confidently. You are more likely to drop something you have not picked up properly.

❖ Extra care must be taken when handling a large or stock sheet piece of glass. Before handling, tap the glass gently with the ball end cutter. If it rattles you may have a "run" or accidental crack in the sheet that can cause the sheet to break apart while you are moving it on the cutting table.

❖ Although you can avoid most accidents by simple precautions, occasionally mistakes are made and a minor injury can result. So always keep a first aid kit handy, and well-stocked with antiseptic cream and sticking plasters.

❖ Always wash your hands thoroughly after using lead, solder and flux, especially if you are planning to handle food.

❖ When soldering and fluxing, it is best to ensure good ventilation by opening a window.

Leading

 There are two parallel techniques used for assembling glasswork. Leading, the traditional method, is often associated with classic stained glass windows, while copper foil – a more contemporary approach – is identified with lampshades. Both systems have their advantages and a working knowledge of each method is essential for glasswork today. Very often people will stay with whatever technique they learned first, thereby setting a limit on the development of their craft.

LEAD CHANNELS

Leading is the traditional framework used to build up windows. Rumor has it that this technique was developed because the early glass makers were not able to produce sheets of glass large enough to fill a window void. Whatever the true origins of this technique, little has changed since the first leaded light was made from small pieces of glass held together with lead channels or cames. A lead came, which is either an H or U shape in profile, is generally available in 4–6 foot lengths. Glass is fitted into the channel of the cames and these are then soldered together at the junctions.

Various sized cames are used for window projects, depending upon both the size of the glass pieces and the size of the window itself. The center of the came is known as the heart. Lead cames are available with either a flat or round surface. Cames come in different widths. The most common widths used are ³⁄₁₆ inch, ¼ inch, ⅜ inch and ½ inch. Deciding which came goes where is determined by a balance of both aesthetics and structure.

Most studios will have a preference for a particular style of leading and we always select "round" lead as it seems to be stronger and less likely to distort while "leading up".

By application, lead cames must be flexible, malleable channels that can be formed around the various shapes of cut glass. Most lead manufactured today is extruded through a metal die and is usually at least 99 per cent pure lead. The first concern of many beginners is how to transport this floppy, bending channel safely home without folding and kinking it into a useless mass of scrap. We have seen extreme cases of people arriving to purchase cames equipped with a 6 foot length of board to keep the cames straight on the journey home. This overcaution is not necessary as all lead is straightened by stretching just prior to use. Ideally, lead should be used directly from the manufacturer's lead boxes. But we have found that coiling the lengths is a perfectly safe and convenient method of transporting small amounts of came for future use.

Lead Working Equipment

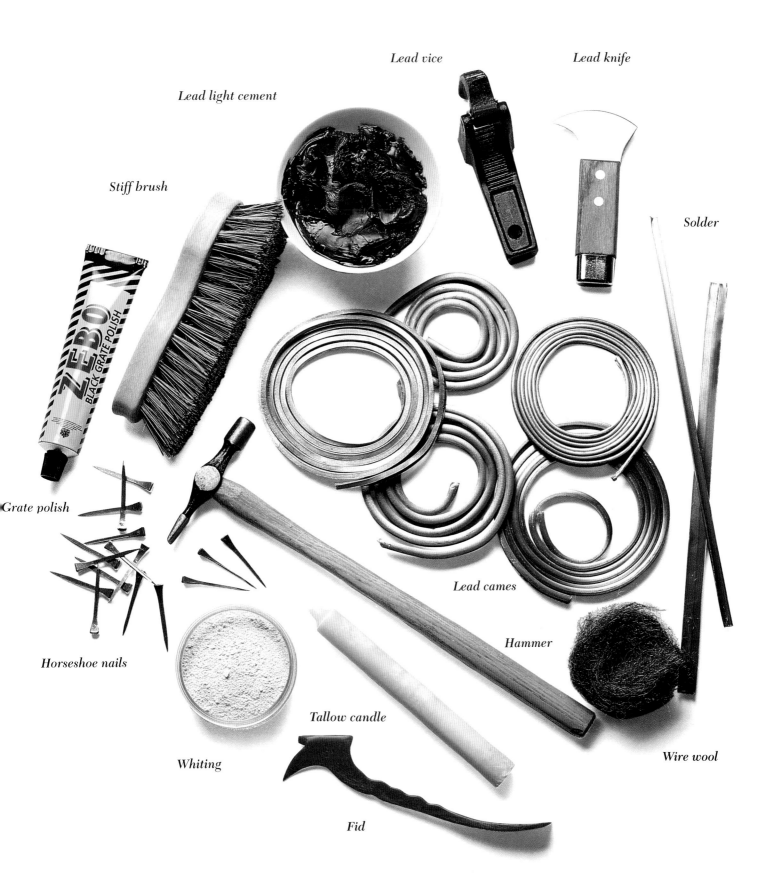

Lead vice

Lead knife

Lead light cement

Stiff brush

Solder

ZEBO
BLACK GRATE POLISH

Grate polish

Lead cames

Hammer

Horseshoe nails

Wire wool

Tallow candle

Whiting

Fid

There are several tools and materials that come into play when leading and this list will be helpful to explain how each fit into the process:

LEAD VICE

The vice is used to hold one end of the channel securely while the other end is pulled firmly to straighten and strengthen the came. Use a pair of pliers to help you: pull just enough to straighten the came without adding more than one inch to the total length. Pull too hard and the came can either slip from the vice or snap in two, sending you backwards to an uncertain fate. Remember that cames are only stretched once just prior to use.

Stretching the came with the lead vice and a pair of pliers.

LATHE OR FID

Available in many shapes, the lathe or fid opens the lead channel, allowing the glass to be positioned within. Cames will distort while being worked into position and the channels must always be reopened to ease leading. After a came has been stretched, run the rounded end inside the channel, flairing it slightly outwards. This tool will wear with use and should be "re-pointed" so that it will continue to reach inside and open the channel. We have found that the best lathes are handmade from a hard wood like ash or oak and personalized to suit the hand.

LEAD KNIFE

Lead knives are used to cut the cames to size while the panel is being leaded together. There are two basic shapes available and which is best is just a matter of preference. The long curved blade of the Don Carlos or the short, rounded blade of the standard knife, both give a firm, crisp cut.

The rounded blade is moved from side to side as pressure is applied downward cutting the came neatly with a minimal amount of distortion. A short putty knife with a rigid, non-flexing blade can be adapted for lead cutting with acceptable results. Most lead knives are available with a weighted end used for tapping horseshoe nails into position. Like any knife, the blade will dull with use and should be periodically re-sharpened on a wet stone. Dull knives tend to crush the lead making it difficult or impossible to work with.

HORSESHOE NAILS

Horseshoe nails are used while leading is in progress to hold the glass and lead in position. The flat sided, sharp nail is less likely to damage the glass or lead than a conventional oval shaped nail and they are easily removed as the leading progresses.

CEMENT

As you will soon notice, the glass will generally fit comfortably into the came leaving a generous gap alongside. Cementing the panel fills this space, making the window strong and weatherproof.

Most studios will purchase a ready made cement especially made for leaded lights. However, this luxury can be avoided by making your own. Numerous recipes are available and ours is but one.

Mix sash putty, white spirit and plaster into a dense, cream-like liquid. Grate some charcoal into a fine powder and add to darken the mixture.

The cement is applied with a stiff brush strong enough to push the mixture into all the recesses of the lead channel.

How long the cement is left to dry on the panel is a matter of temperature and the type of cement itself. During warm weather, cement can set in a few hours, making removal the next day a nightmare of epic proportions. The cement should never be allowed to set firmly on the glass and lead.

WHITING

The whiting, or powdered chalk, is used to absorb the excess oil from the cement, allowing the panel to become dry and clean. A softer brush is used to remove the cement and whiting.

SOLDER

An alloy of two metals, lead and tin, solder is melted with a soldering iron and is used for both copper foil and lead came projects. Sold by weight and graded by the ratio of lead to tin, we recommend using a 50:50 mix. Solder with a higher tin content will melt at a lower temperature and finish with a more silvery appearance.

Solder with a resin or flux core is intended only for electrical repair work and is best avoided. The same goes for plumber's solder, which is temptingly inexpensive because of the low tin content, but extremely unworkable when soldered to anything but copper piping.

Copper Foil

 Copper foil is a thin tape with an adhesive back that is wrapped around the glass. The foiled pieces of glass are then soldered together in strong, delicate shapes or patterns.

When compared to lead cames, copper foil is a simpler technique requiring less steps and fewer materials to complete a project. However, the main attraction to foil work is its tremendous versatility in tackling a wide range of projects, from small window hangings to lampshades.

The copper foil method is attributed to the inventiveness of Louis Comfort Tiffany, whose name has always been associated with the delicate "Tiffany" lampshades and windows of the late 19th century. Not content with the heavy, one dimensional qualities of traditional lead cames, Tiffany's craftsmen cut thin strips of copper which were wrapped around the glass and then soldering together in complex patterns and shapes.

Like the lead came, the question of which size foil to use is a common question when beginning a project. One of the advantages of copper foil is the delicacy which can be achieved and we always use as narrow a foil as possible. However, narrow foil is more time-consuming to apply and is not suitable for all projects. Lampshades or windows with large pieces of glass will require wider foil which is stronger and which will maintain a rigid shape. Although most machine-made glass is ⅛ inch thick, antique or handmade glass can vary in thickness even within the sheet itself which can necessitate using two different foil sizes on a single piece.

Various sizes of copper foil tape with hand crimpers and burnishers.

Copper foil is conveniently available in sealed bags ranging in size from $\frac{5}{32}$ inch to ½ inch widths suitable for all types of colored glass. The few specialized tools used for copper foil were devised to remove some of the tedium of wrapping large quantities of glass in preparation for assembly.

FOILING MACHINE

A grooved, hard rubber roller centers and wraps the foil as the glass is pushed around. Although this type of machine requires practise, eventually the glass can be wrapped with much greater speed and accuracy than by hand. The machines are generally supplied with three interchangeable rollers – $\frac{3}{16}$, $\frac{7}{32}$ and ¼ inch – being the most commonly used widths.

Electrically powered foiling machines are quicker still. The rubber wheel, activated by a foot switch, is driven by an electric motor.

FOIL CRIMPER

Whether you use a foiling machine or hand foil each piece, the foil must be folded and smoothed on to the sides of the glass to achieve a neat, strong bond. Although foiling machines often claim to burnish each piece as it is wrapped, in reality the foiled edges must be turned down or smoothed as a separate step. A crimper has a thin, flexible groove that – when run around the foiled edge – presses both these edges smooth against the glass with one action.

A flat piece of wood will also crimp the foil, one side at a time.

FINISHING PATINAS

After you have completed the assembly of your lampshade or panel made with the copper foil technique there are several alternatives for finishing the soldered areas. Solder, like most metals, will oxidize and discolor in time leaving a dull gray finish. High tin content solder will retain its lustre if treated with metal polish and some pieces do benefit aesthetically from this treatment. However, we have found that the dramatic contrast of glass and soldered lines is further highlighted by darkening the solder with a patina. All patinas work best when applied to the solder immediately after the project is complete. If you wait even a few hours, the solder will begin to oxidize, requiring a quick rub down with a fine grade wire wool or a wash with hot soapy water to achieve a bright finish. A patina finish will also brighten if rubbed with metal polish.

COPPER SULPHATE CRYSTALS: A patina that leaves the soldered lines a coppery color. Dissolve one tablespoon of the crystals in half a cup of hot water.

BLACK-IT AND COPPER-BRIGHT SOLUTION: These two chemicals are available as a pre-mixed solution and will give a stronger and darker finish than copper sulphate. Black-it contains a trace amount of selenium oxide, an extremely strong chemical which demands care when used. It will blacken solder. Copper-bright turns the solder a copper color. Always wear rubber gloves when working with any of the finishing patinas.

ABOVE *A copper foiling machine. This is worth investing in if you plan to make a lot of copper foil projects.*

BELOW *Finishing patinas, clockwise from top: black-it, copper-bright and copper sulphate crystals.*

Soldering

To assemble the pieces of glass – whether they are leaded or foiled – you will need to use solder and a soldering iron. Soldering irons, like pliers, tend to be a household item that lie in wait, quietly rusting, until a small bit of electrical repair work requires them to be retrieved from the bottom of the tool drawer. Unfortunately, the iron that many of us are able to borrow from a friend or locate in a drawer is seldom up to the job for soldering for glasswork. We have found that people who have trouble soldering are usually working with a tool that isn't appropriate for the job.

Nowadays, as a matter of convenience and safety, most studios work with electric rather than gas heated irons. The gas heats up the tip of the iron with an open flame and the iron requires a cylinder which takes up space and may well be against safety regulations.

SOLDERING IRONS AND HOW TO USE THEM

Irons of less than 75 watt do not retain enough heat to melt the amounts of solder that you will be using. When soldering, the iron is in constant use and the process will soon begin to dissipate the heat that has built up in the tip of the iron. Small irons with little heat retention will lose heat so quickly that the solder will stop flowing and become tacky and sluggish, making joints weak and messy.

Irons of over 150 watt tend to be just too speedy for most work and have a tendency to burn or melt everything they come into contact with. Large wattage irons can be regulated by switching the power off when excessive heat causes meltdown, but this procedure is usually forgotten and you are left wondering why the iron has gone cold.

There are available, at a price, irons that seem to be made especially for glasswork that contain a temperature control unit built into the handle. The temperature is regulated by replaceable tips of various heat ranges and size. One temperature control iron in the 100–200 watt range can be used for delicate or heavy work by a simple exchange of tips.

At one time, irons were only available with massive copper tips that corroded and required constant re-shaping with metal files. Most irons are now available with a iron-coated or plated tip giving a long life and ease of use. For most work, a screwdriver shaped tip measuring about ¼ inch at its working end will give smooth, neat joints. Any metal that is constantly heated, cooled and exposed to corrosive chemicals will soon show wear. No matter what iron you use, remove the tip frequently to prevent it from seizing in the barrel and eventually ruining the iron.

Impurities in solder and lead will cause carbon deposits to build up on the tip surface greatly decreasing its ability to transfer heat to the work. Allow the iron to heat up to its working temperature and wipe the tip with a chemical cleaner or damp sponge until the tip is shiny. This process, known as "tinning", is repeated whenever the tip is discolored with black carbon deposits. The coated tip, unlike the old solid copper ones, can never be filed or re-shaped. Once the coating is damaged, the tip will rapidly begin to deteriorate. The manufacturer's instructions will always state something like: "Do not file coated tip" and you can be sure this is a true piece of advice.

After all the thought and deliberation about wattage, tip shape, coated or copper, temperature control etc, there is one last item that is often overlooked. Buy a metal stand that is large enough to keep the iron from rolling off the table, setting fire to the carpet and perhaps spreading to the rest of your home. In addition to melting solder, irons are also excellent incendiary devices and when given the opportunity will burn any nearby combustible.

There is a range of soldering irons available for glasswork. Be sure to purchase a metal stand too, as soldering irons can quickly burn neighboring items if left lying by themselves on a worktable.

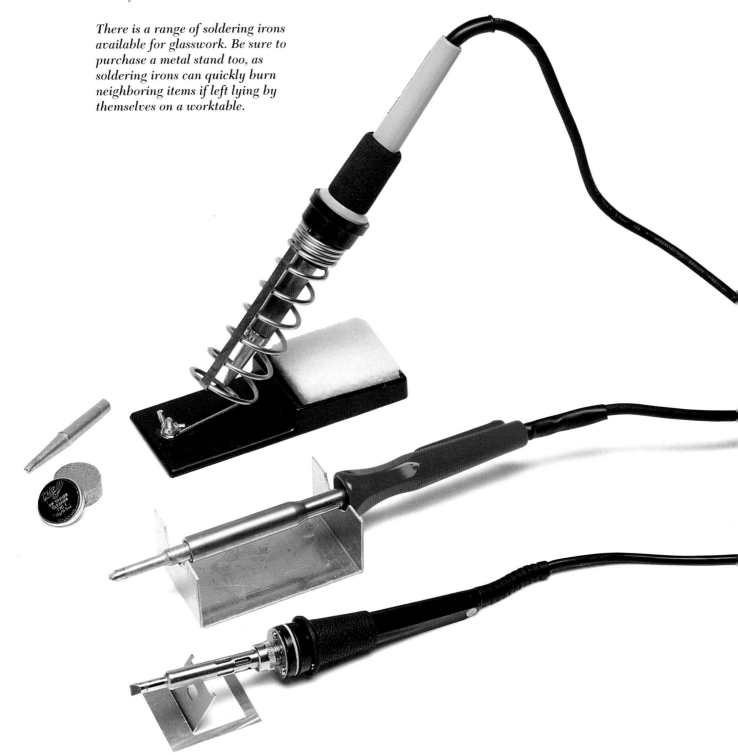

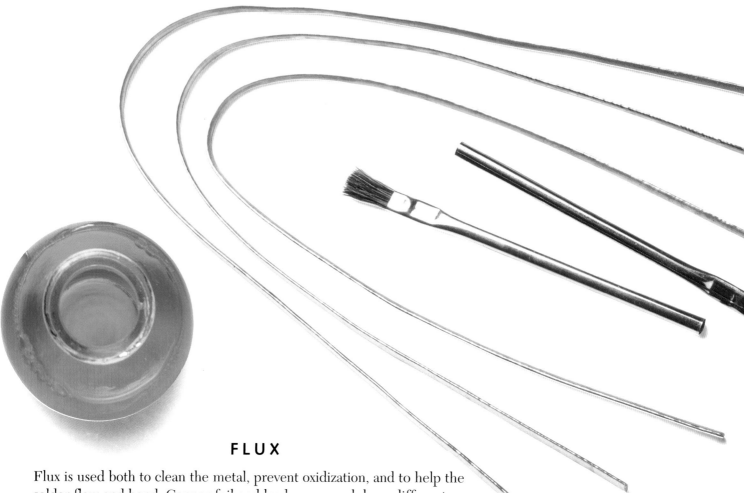

FLUX

Flux is used both to clean the metal, prevent oxidization, and to help the solder flow and bond. Copper foil and lead cames each have different soldering requirements and there are two distinct fluxes for each task.

Appearing like a candle without a wick, **tallow** is a natural flux used when soldering on lead cames. Although tallow will clean the lead joint when heated by the iron, use a soft wire brush or wire wool just prior to fluxing to remove any oxidization that may have occurred. This will provide clean, shiny joints ready for soldering. Lead cames that are stored wrapped in newspaper or boxed will remain free of oxidization and will be easier to solder.

Unlike lead cames that are soldered only at junctions, copper foil projects are soldered along the entire seam and require a different flux. Just like cames, soldering is always a quicker, smoother process if the foil has not been allowed to discolor or oxidize. Rolls of copper foil that are stored in the original packaging will remain clean and free of oxidization and ready for use. Don't leave foiled glass lying around for too long before soldering, as the foil will tarnish.

The active ingredient in most commercial fluxes is zinc chloride, a corrosive, toxic chemical that while being an effective flux, is a very unpleasant material to work with. We only use non-toxic, water-based fluxes that do not emit harmful fumes or corrode the soldering tips. Use sparingly and only flux the areas you will be soldering immediately, as flux evaporates and leaves residues on the foil which will affect the process.

As bottles of flux have a habit of frequently falling over and soaking everything around, pour a small amount into an open top container for immediate use and keep the rest safely bottled.

Solder, brushes and flux for use with copper foil work.

How to Solder

Soldering affects both the appearance and strength of a piece and is an important aspect of any project. Whether you are working with copper foil or lead, your soldering success will depend on having an iron of adequate wattage with a clean, tinned tip ready to melt solder. Turn the iron on and when hot wipe with either a damp sponge or chemical tip cleaner to remove blackened deposits. Brush the tip with flux and then melt a touch of solder on to it. The iron should readily melt the solder so that the working area of the tip is covered with a shiny coating of solder. Irons that are blackened by the impurities from lead and solder will not transmit heat efficiently to the working area, regardless of the wattage.

LEAD CHANNELS

Small gaps where the channels meet can be filled or packed by cutting off the bottom of a small wedge of lead and inserting the "T" into the gap. Once you are satisfied that all the gaps have been filled, it is often helpful to give the joints a quick clean with a fine wire brush to remove any oxidization. Hold the solder on the joint and allow the iron to melt a neat pool of solder. A few moments is usually long enough to solder the lead into a strong, neat joint. If the iron is not hot enough the solder will appear lumpy and irregular, while too hot and the iron can melt away the lead channel itself. Be careful! Don't be concerned about the heat of the iron cracking the glass.

COPPER FOIL

Copper foil is soldered along the entire length of the adjoining sections of glass. As with lead, copper foil that has been oxidized will be difficult to solder and we advise keeping your foiled pieces protected in a plastic bag if there is a delay of a day or more before you are ready to solder. There are three soldering techniques employed when working with copper foil.

HOW TO SOLDER COPPER FOIL

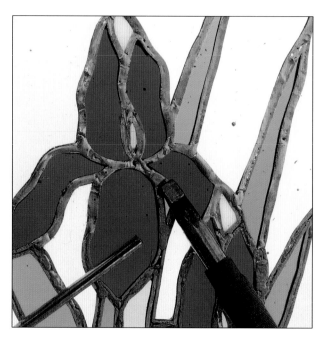

TACK SOLDERING: *To prevent pieces moving out of position by the very action of soldering, use a small blob of solder to hold the glass in place. Apply flux with a brush at key junctions and then melt a small amount of solder to hold the pieces together. Tack soldering is also essential with three-dimensional projects to hold the shape temporarily in position before going on to the next step.*

TINNING OR FLAT SOLDERING: *The inside seams of most copper foil projects are soldered with just a smooth or flat seam of solder. Flux the copper foil with a brush and begin soldering by flowing just enough solder to coat the seam and fill in any gaps. Although you can form a "bead" of solder directly to the copper foil, sometimes it is more useful to tin the seams first and then to bead the outside areas afterwards on top of the tinned seams. This is particularly advisable when you are building up three dimensional projects.*

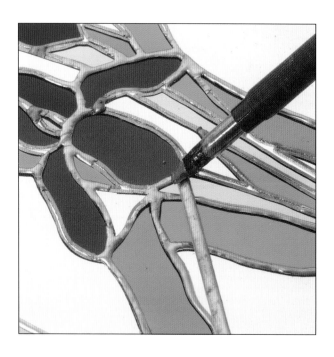

BEAD SOLDERING: *This process is generally applied to the outside of the finished project. Apply flux to the complete seam and slowly move the iron along the seam while feeding in solder to either the top or side of the tip. Work slowly, moving the iron only as fast as it is able to melt the solder. You should allow the solder to build up until it forms a domed or rounded smooth seam. Only flux a small area at a time, as the flux itself will evaporate. Moving the iron too quickly is the most common problem for beginners, and learning to form a smooth, neat bead can sometimes take a little practice.*

Glass Painting

 Glass painting has been used to illustrate and decorate leaded glass windows throughout the centuries. Exquisite artistry created draping folds of fabric, faces rich with expression and flora and fauna alike.

Painting on glass is an exacting technique and is very different from many other forms of pictorial painting. Paint for glass is a mixture of powdered oxides which are ground and mixed with water and gum arabic. Much of the technique lies in not just applying the paint but also removing it to create texture and shading. The finished work is fired in a kiln to fuse the paint to the glass.

EQUIPMENT

There are certain tools that are required for glass painting. However you can improvise and in some cases ordinary artists' brushes will work if you are unable to purchase the specialized ones.

Not all glass artists have a kiln of their own. Professional studios will often hire their kiln for an hourly fee. Or contact a local college and enquire if there is a kiln available on the same basis.

GLASS PALETTE

This is to provide a surface for mixing the paints. You will need a square of thick, clear glass preferably sandblasted to provide an abrasive surface for mixing the paint powder. A palette knife is useful for mixing the paint.

Gum arabic

Stippler

Hog hair brush

Trace brushes

Mop brushes

Palette knife

Badger brush

BRUSHES

LINER, RIGGER OR TRACER: Long-haired brushes which are soft, flexible and have a slender point. They are used with trace paint for tracing outlines and delicate work.

MOP OR WASH BRUSH: A round soft brush for holding enough paint to apply a wash.

BADGER: A thick, very soft, long-haired brush for matting or shading color (see below).

HOGHAIR BRUSH OR SCRUB: A stiff short-haired brush for stippling paint before it has been fired.

OTHER EQUIPMENT

TOOTHPICKS: or sharp-pointed bamboo sticks are useful for picking away the paint.

ARM REST: For resting your wrist while leaving your hand free over the glass, you will do well to employ an arm support. This can easily be made from a narrow strip of wood with a small block of wood glued to each end.

MATERIALS

TRACE PAINT

A dark paint used for outlines and details in line form. If used correctly it can block out light completely. Trace paint is mixed with water and gum arabic. The gum arabic is a setting medium and enables the paint to adhere to the glass.

Trace paint is applied with a tracer or rigger. You must apply the paint in one continuous stroke with the brush. Once the paint has dried (which is very quickly) you must not go back and apply more paint over the line. If you do, it will "fry" when it is fired, ie the two overlying areas of paint will separate when heated and bubble. You must also not retouch the line that has been painted. Once the trace line is dry you can use a toothpick or bamboo stick to remove excess paint. Literally scrape off what you don't want. Trace paint is fired at about 1150°F. This will probably vary from kiln to kiln.

SHADING COLOR

Used for shadowing, shading color creates tone and texture. It is generally mixed with water and a drop of gum arabic and is applied with a soft brush or "mop" over the entire area on which you are working. It is then stippled or worked on with various brushes to create a particular tone, shadow or texture.

Many different effects can be created with shading color once it is applied. It is also applied over trace paint and usually after the trace paint has been fired. Shading color can be used alone and is fired in the same way as trace paint. Shading color and trace paint fire to a lighter tone.

SILVER STAIN

Silver stain is the misleading name given to glass stains that produce yellow to amber colors after firing. Stain will change the color of glass, unlike paint which simply covers it. Stain is mixed with water and is usually applied to the back of the glass – the opposite side to trace paint and shading color.

Silver stain contains silver nitrate and has corrosive properties. Don't use the same brushes and palette as you do for paints. Always wash the brushes and equipment immediately, and avoid contact with skin. Some glass will not accept silver stain so care must be taken when choosing the type of glass to be stained. A good idea is to test a piece first and keep a record for future reference. Stains fire at approximately 1110°F.

Always clean the glass thoroughly before painting with a little of the paint itself. Allow to dry then wipe the paint off with a clean rag.

FIRING COLORS IN A KILN

Kiln working and painting is a specialized subject and here we are only able to give a very basic introduction to their use. If you are interested in finding out more about this subject we suggest you consult a book that deals only with painting on glass.

The high temperature used in the kiln allows the paint and glass to fire together forming a single decorative surface which is permanent. There are many types of glass kilns available, from small units that fire single pieces of glass to large batch type kilns capable of firing many pieces in one go. All glass kilns must have a controllable temperature range up to a minimum of 1200°F.

We have always used a propane gas-fired top loader which has proved to be efficient, quick and trouble-free. Electric kilns are also widely used, although we have found them to require more time to complete a firing cycle. Our kiln has a digital temperature control unit which allows us to program a firing cycle. The pieces are placed painted side up on to a smooth, level bed of whiting (calcium carbonate or plaster of Paris) which prevents the glass fusing with the kiln itself. After we have selected the appropriate temperature the kiln is fired. At the end of the firing we simply turn off the kiln and allow the glass to cool slowly or anneal. Do not open the kiln while it is still hot, or you will be greeted by the gentle pop of cracking glass as the cold air rushes in.

Sandblasting

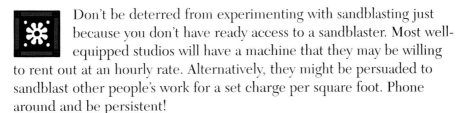

Don't be deterred from experimenting with sandblasting just because you don't have ready access to a sandblaster. Most well-equipped studios will have a machine that they may be willing to rent out at an hourly rate. Alternatively, they might be persuaded to sandblast other people's work for a set charge per square foot. Phone around and be persistent!

The sandblasting unit consists of four basic elements which all work together. The air compressor is the motor of the unit and provides compressed air to the sand mixing unit. The pressurized sand is then forced through a flexible pipe into a sealed cabinet where it exits through a gun fitted with a small nozzle. An extractor fan attached to the cabinet removes excess sand and maintains clear visibility while sandblasting.

Insert your hands into the long rubber gloves that are sealed where they enter the cabinet to position the glass and control the sand jet.

RESIST

The preparation and application of the resist is the main skill of sandblasting. The resist protects the glass surface from the abrasive power of the pressurized sand. Areas left exposed to the sand jet will be abraded or frosted. Transparent resist is a heavy grade of adhesive film with a paper backing that is peeled away. We have used ordinary sticky-back vinyl with good results, although the clear resist is both stronger and easier for transferring a design on to the glass.

Glass Appliqué

 Glass appliqué is similar to fabric appliqué, where a pattern or picture is built up from small scraps of material sewn on to a larger piece.

The application of glass on to glass is a technique that involves neither lead nor copper foil. Basically, scraps of glass are glued on to a glass panel and the gaps in between are grouted. The glass pieces can be literally scrap shapes, or you can cut them according to your design. The end result can be abstract or you can form a definite picture or pattern with the glass.

Apart from the obvious glass cutting tools, wet and dry paper for polishing the edges of cut pieces, you will need silicone adhesive, and black Universal stainer to mix with white interior filler to form a "grout".

CHAPTER THREE

Designing Stained Glass

❖ ❖ ❖

Designing your own stained glass patterns can be immensely satisfying and is not as difficult as you might think. To begin with, most people gain their experience from copying ideas and using templates in books. The next step is to design your own patterns and pictures. Inspiration for design concepts can come from almost anywhere: books, magazines, the natural world around you, a child's drawing – the list is virtually endless. This chapter looks at how to translate these ideas into an actual stained glass project, to avoid certain pitfalls and to produce an item of which you are proud and pleased.

There are many stained glass pattern books on the market for beginners and advanced students alike. There are also many books with pictures of contemporary and traditional stained glass windows that will give you inspiration. However, most people will find themselves developing their own ideas as their skills improve and, inevitably wanting to create their own designs.

When designing or developing concepts to be made from glass, certain limitations are imposed due to the restrictions of the material. Sometimes this can work to your advantage because you are forced to think further than just the picture on the paper. Adding extra lines or sections of glass to balance the strength of the project could enhance the design unexpectedly.

With lead and copper foil being the "skeleton" of the piece in terms of holding the glass together, these lines should be considered an integral part of the design and can be utilized as such.

Ideas can, and will come from many different sources. Consider adapting a drawing or a design from paintings, interesting graphics, architectural details, magazine features, depending on your particular style or taste and whether the image is figurative or linear. Color balance will play an important part in the appearance and effect of the finished piece. When you are working with transparent glass, hold it up to the light and consider the color, texture and "light play" as the sun shines through the glass.

This fabulous parrot was based on a photograph which was stylized to create the mirror design. The wall lights were then conceived to complement the mirror. All the items were made using the versatile copper foil technique.

LYNETTE WRIGLEY

LEFT *Nature again is the inspiration for this beautiful window and the design has been translated using the glass appliqué technique.*

FROEBEL COLLEGE, LONDON

Most studios will have a light box on which to lay pieces of glass to see how one color appears against another. This works well for both opalescent and transparent glass. A light box can also be useful to trace the pattern through on to the glass and eliminate the need for templates.

For transparent glass, an easel is the most effective method of displaying your choice of colors, but as this is a large piece of equipment to have in your home, you may prefer to stick small pieces of glass with adhesive putty to a window pane. This will provide the same answers and will enable you to see where one color may overpower another.

Once you have formulated a concept for a design, draw it out on paper. Measure a perimeter and plan the design within it. Look at it and decide if some of the shapes are too small or impossible to cut. Alter it accordingly. Keep the design simple and avoid any difficult cuts. You will build up more confidence by designing and executing a simple pattern, rather than overwhelming yourself with a complicated one.

Making a Selection

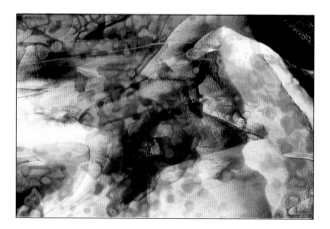

A mottled opal for a fish pool or green foliage?

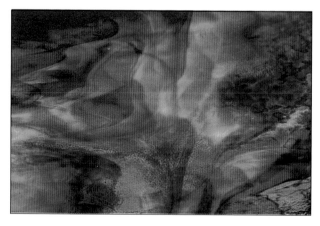

A fabulous fiery sunset.

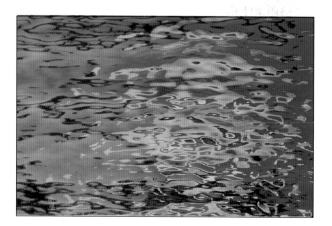

Water glass is an obvious choice for anything watery.

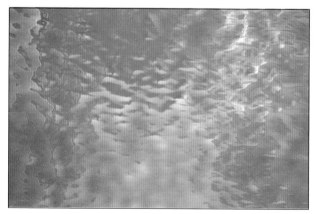

The perfect selection for sky.

While designing the panel, consider its strength. A design with smaller pieces of glass will be stronger than a panel with a few large sections that do not intersect. Avoid a long line of glass that travels from one side of the panel to the other. Unless divided in some way with your design line, a narrow section of glass will be a vulnerable part of the panel and could break.

Once you have modified your drawing for cutting and you are satisfied with the effect, ink it in and make at least two or three copies. Whether you are working in lead or foil, you will always need one copy for cutting from and one copy to check that your pieces fit. It is important that you work in a sense of order with glass. Unnecessary breakages and minor cuts can occur if your table is messy.

Consider the streaks and color variation in the choice of glass available. Use these selections to your advantage. Illustrate a cloudy sky with a streaky blue, mottled green may suit foliage on a tree. Water glass could not be a better choice than for water.

CHAPTER FOUR

Projects using copper foil

✦ ✦ ✦

Copper foil is a versatile medium for holding pieces of glass together. Its flexibility from both the practical point of view and the opportunity for design gives the stained glass worker enormous potential. Tiny pieces of glass can be wrapped with the foil and soldered together to form the most intricate details. Three dimensional forms can be developed with more dexterity than with lead.

Some glass artists have a personal preference for working with either lead or foil, but when choosing to make items such as lampshades, boxes or jewelry, copper foil would be the practical choice.

Cathedral Mirror

YOU WILL NEED

+ ⅛ inch mirrored glass
+ 2 colors of rolled cathedral glass
+ felt tip pen
+ glass cutter
+ grozing pliers
+ carborundum stone
+ ⁷⁄₃₂ copper foil
+ fid
+ solder
+ soldering iron
+ flux and brush
+ black patina
+ picture wire for hanging

1 *Make three copies of the pattern on page 144 and draw in the external and internal lines with a fine felt tip pen.*

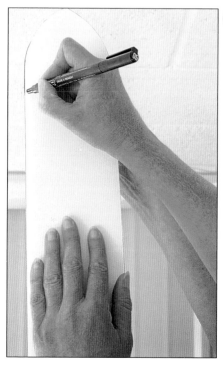

2 *Cut out the central arched panel and place it on to the reflective side of the mirror. Place it slightly inside the edge of the mirror and draw around it with the felt tip pen. Score and cut the mirror as you would for glass.*

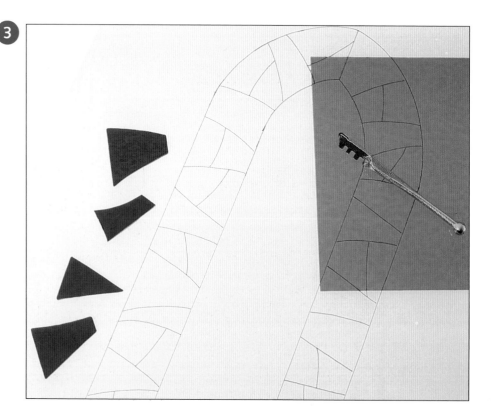

3 *Lay the chosen colored glass on the pattern and cut out the pieces.*

4 Use the pliers to help to break apart the scored pieces. Hold the fingers and thumb close to the score with one hand and the pliers close to the score with the other.

5 Lay out all the cut pieces on to the pattern. Check each piece fits correctly and then rub the edges with the carborundum stone.

6 After washing and drying all the pieces to remove glass dust, wrap each piece in the copper foil.

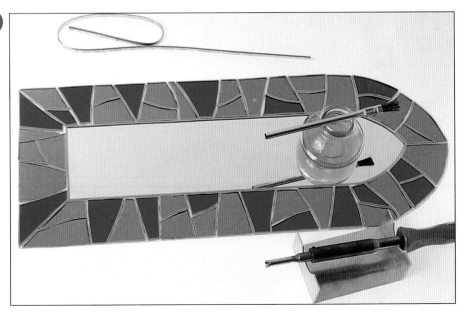

7 Lay the foiled mirror and glass pieces carefully on to the pattern. Double check everything is in place and switch on the soldering iron in preparation for tack soldering. Apply flux where the seams and mirror meet.

8 *With the hot iron, melt a small amount of solder on to the fluxed areas. Tack solder the pieces in position; this will prevent the glass from moving around on the pattern.*

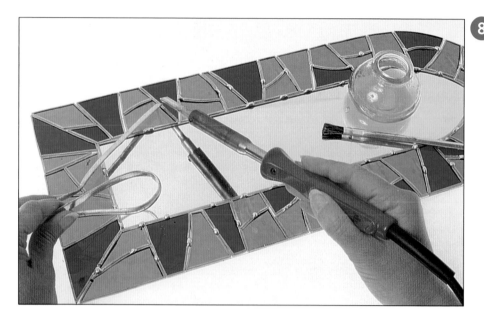

9 *Apply flux once again, but this time to an entire seam. Melt the solder with the iron and allow enough solder to flow to form a smooth raised (beaded) seam.*

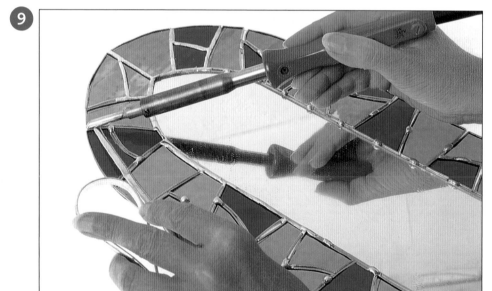

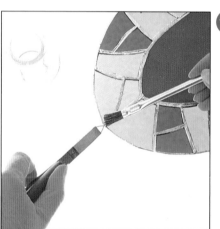

10 *To make a hanging loop, form a 'U' shape with some brass or copper wire and flux the central vertical seam.*

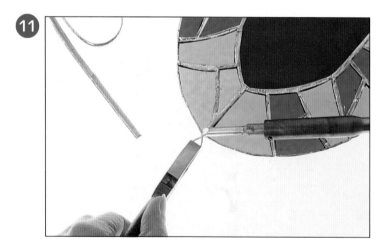

11 *Attach the loop by holding it with the pliers and placing it on to the seam. Melt a drop of solder on to the loop; turn the mirror over and attach it in the same way on the other side.*

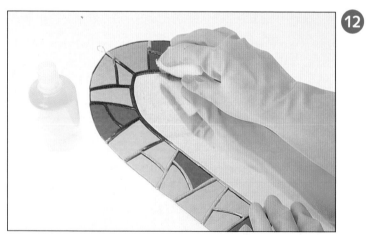

12 *Wearing protective gloves, apply some patina to the soldered seams. Rub gently with a sponge over the solder. Wash the mirror in hot soapy water to finish.*

Each section of this leaded panel was copied from a medieval window. The artist used trace and matt paints to achieve these effects.

JUDITH SOVIN

An autonomous leaded panel displays a fine example of painting, silver staining and acid etching.

JUDITH SOVIN

*A painted and
leaded medieval
window copied
from the St
Eustace window in
Chartres, France.*

JUDITH SOVIN

Wild Irises Panel

YOU WILL NEED

- various colors of antique Polish tatra glass
- glass cutter
- grozing and running pliers
- electric ginder or carborundum stone
- ⁷⁄₃₂ copper foil
- fid
- solder
- soldering iron
- flux and brush
- patina

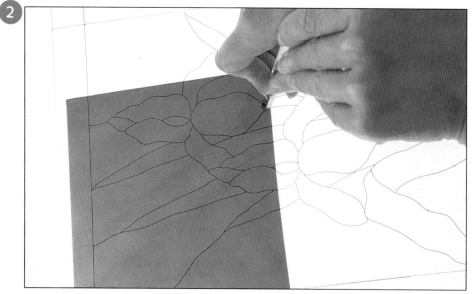

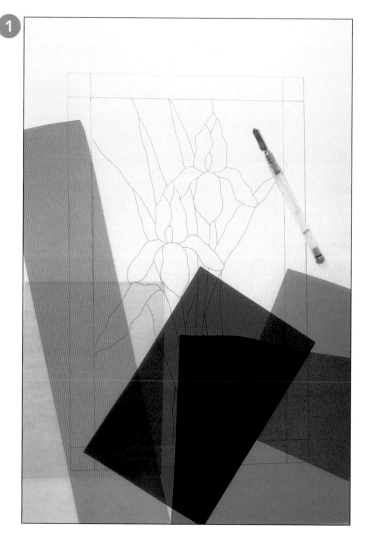

1 *Compare the various colors of glass for balance and harmony.*

2 *The glass is transparent so it can be laid directly on to the design to be cut. (The pattern appears on page 145.) Remember to always make at least two copies of the design: one to cut from and one to lay the pieces on for fitting. Cut the shapes from an area that will limit wastage. Allow a small margin from the shape and the edge of the glass. Start the score from just inside the edge of the glass.*

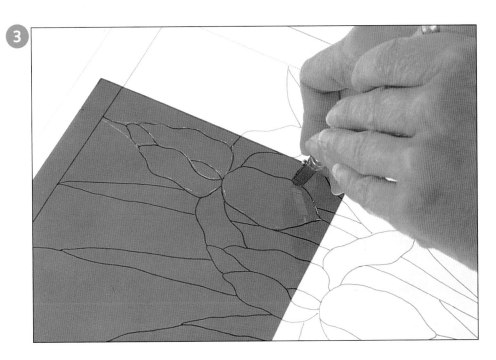

3 Score several pieces ready for breaking.

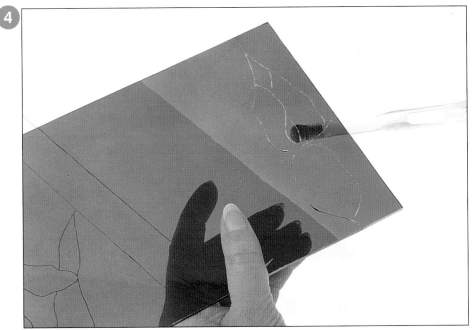

4 Using the ball end of the glass cutter, tap underneath the scored line to assist a tricky curved line to break.

5 Break the pieces with the pliers.

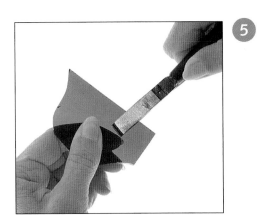

6 Hold the glass firmly with the fingers and thumb of the other hand.

7 Use the pliers to groze off sharp points.

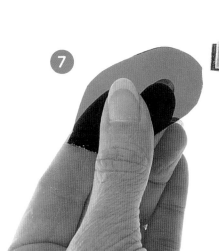

8 *Grind the edges of the glass on the electric grinding machine. Check that it is filled with water for lubricating the wheel. (If you don't have access to an electric grinder, use a carborundum stone.)*

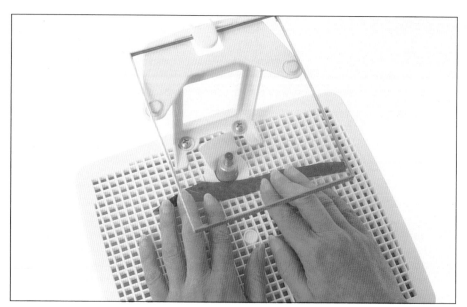

9 *As the borders are long, narrow strips, you will need to use the straight edge to cut them.*

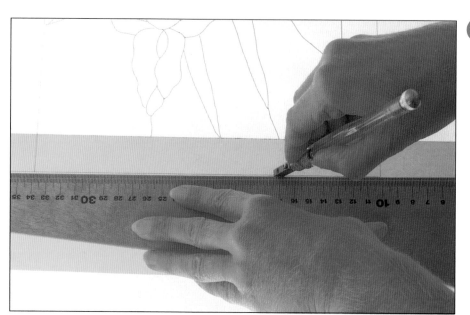

10 *The running pliers are useful to help break these long straight lines. Place the pliers with the raised section under the score and press the pliers together.*

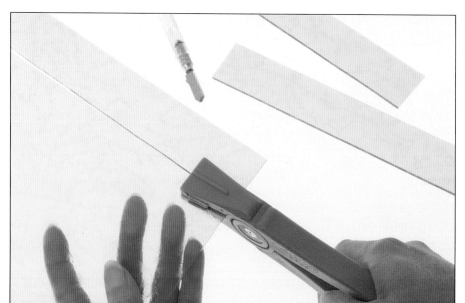

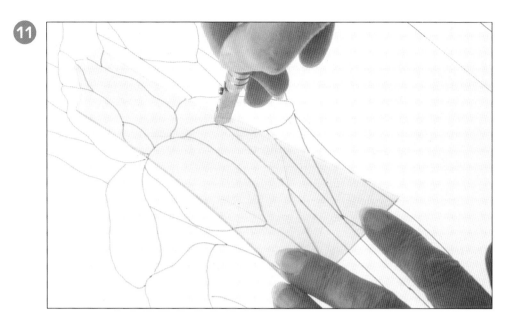

11 *Score the yellow glass following the direction of the vertical lines and then score the curves. Break the pieces with the pliers. Grind all the edges smooth.*

12 *Wash all the pieces before foiling each one.*

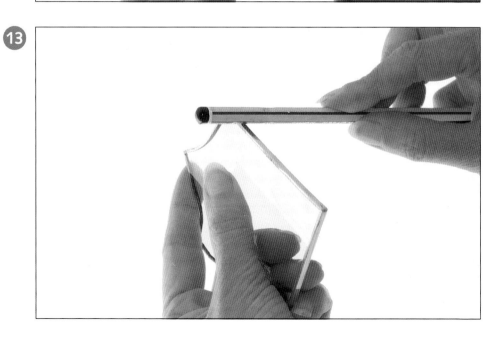

13 *Rub the foil down on to the glass. If you don't have a fid or crimper, use a small piece of wood or a pencil.*

14 *Continue to do this, flattening the foil folded on to the sides of the glass and rubbing it down well.*

15 *Assemble the copper foiled pieces and apply the flux. Tack solder the panel together to prevent the pieces moving about.*

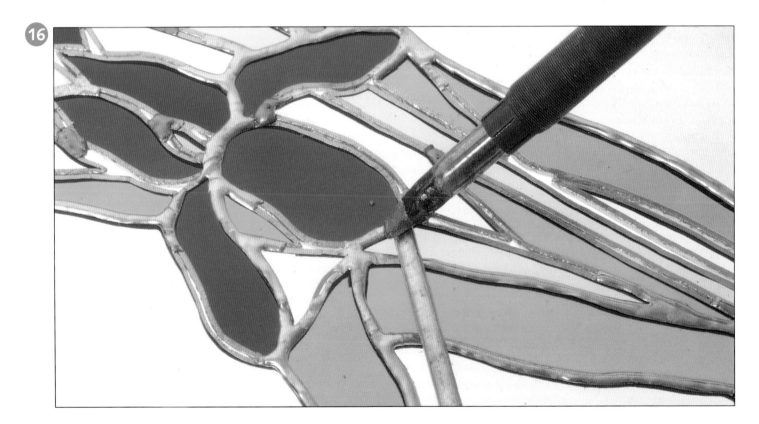

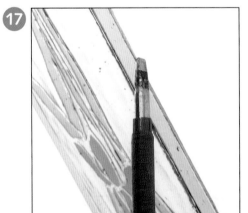

16 *Apply more flux and bead solder the front side of the panel. Turn the panel over and tin the back.*

17 *Hold the panel in a vertical position to tin the edges. Apply patina to the panel with a sponge and then wash it thoroughly with hot water and detergent.*

This autonomous leaded panel uses reeded glass and primary colors.

MATHEW LLOYD
WINDER

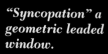

"Syncopation" a geometric leaded window.

MATHEW LLOYD
WINDER

"Phototropism"

MATHEW LLOYD
WINDER

*This leaded
window uses over
20 different types
of glass.*

MATHEW LLOYD
WINDER

Fan Lamp

YOU WILL NEED

- ✤ pale amber opal glass
- ✤ blue wispy opal glass
- ✤ felt tip pen
- ✤ glass cutter
- ✤ grozing pliers
- ✤ carborundum stone
- ✤ ⁷⁄₃₂ copper foil
- ✤ fid
- ✤ solder
- ✤ soldering iron
- ✤ flux and brush
- ✤ copper sulphate solution
- ✤ fan lamp base (from stained glass suppliers)

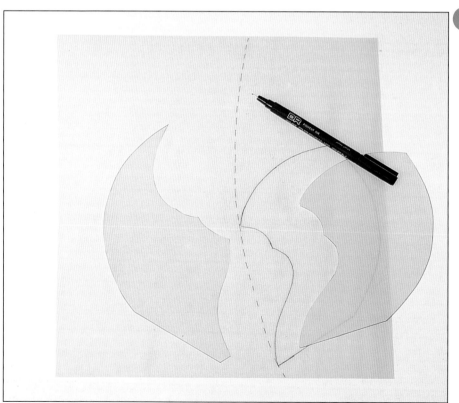

1 Make three copies of the pattern (on page 146) and cut one out for templates.

2 Lay the templates on the glass and trace around them with a felt tip pen. (Take care to observe the flow of the pattern on the glass and match it when you lay down the opposite template.)

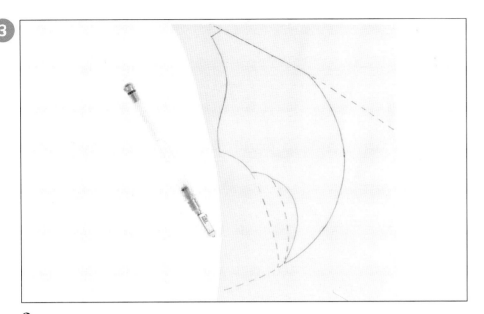

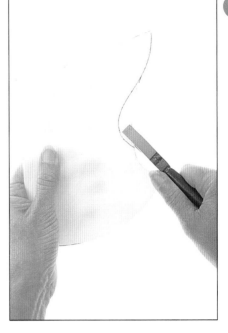

3 Start scoring the shape following the suggested dotted guidelines. Break these off with the pliers and then make several scores into the curved section.

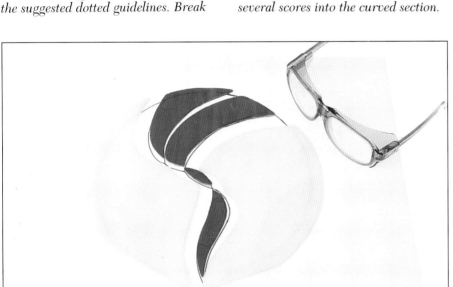

4 Put the pliers next to the score and start to break these pieces away with a firm pulling motion.

5 Score and cut the darker glass. If you have chosen a glass that is not transparent you will need templates as guides for cutting. Grind the edges of all the pieces and wash them ready for foiling.

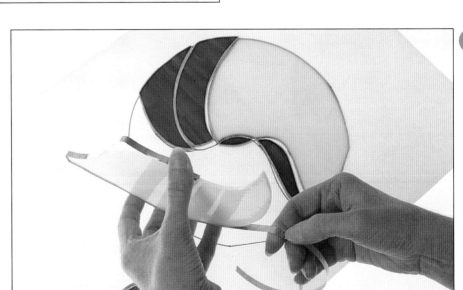

6 Foil each piece, carefully placing the glass in the center of the adhesive tape and leaving an equal amount exposed on either side. Fold the sides of the tape down and rub or "crimp" them on to the glass.

7 *Flux and tack the foiled pieces together.*

8 *Now flux and solder along the length of the seams. Bead solder the front then turn over and tin the back.*

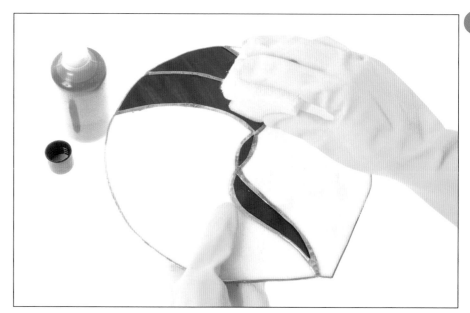

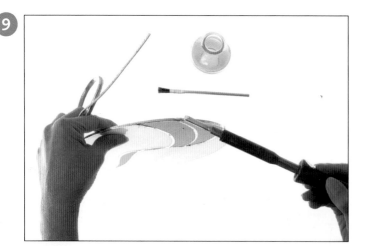

9 *Flux the sides and hold in an upright position while soldering. The sides will not require too much solder, just a light tinned coat.*

10 *After washing the panel, wear some protective gloves and apply some copper sulphate solution with a sponge. Finish with a final wash in warm, soapy water.*

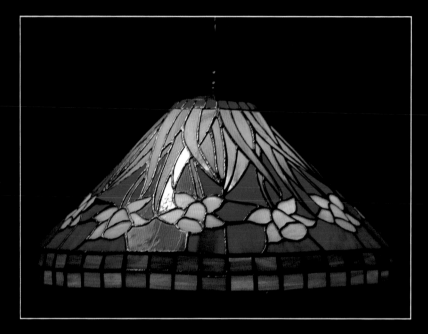

A Tiffany-style copper foiled lampshade made on a styrofoam form.

LYNETTE WRIGLEY

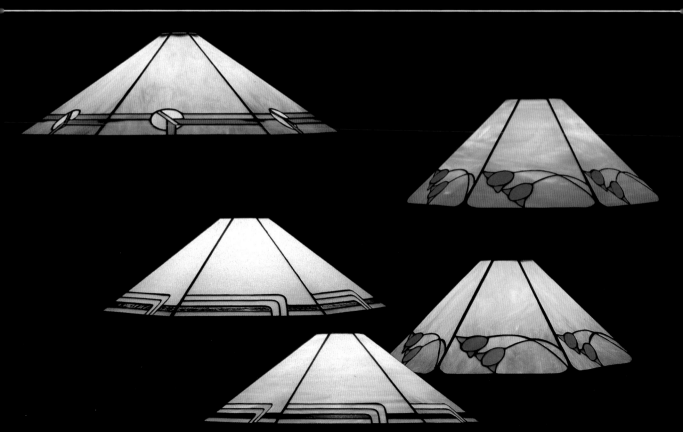

Flat-panelled Lamp

YOU WILL NEED

- various opalescent glass: pale amber, red, blue and green
- pencil and ruler
- glass cutter
- grozing and running pliers
- carborundum stone
- $\frac{7}{32}$ copper foil
- fid
- solder
- soldering iron
- flux and brush
- patina
- vase cap and hoop
- bulb holder and chain
- lamp base

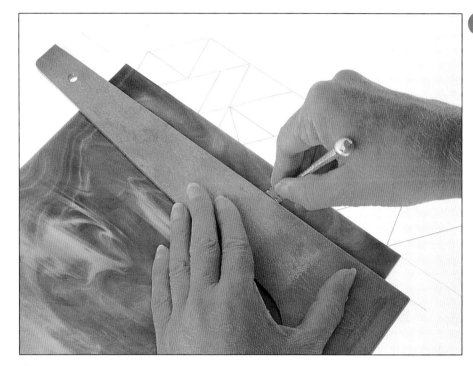

1

1 *Following the pattern on page 00, extend the diagonal lines with a pencil and ruler, as shown. Use these lines as a guide to measure the width of each* strip to be cut. Align the glass, and use a straight edge. Position the wheel of the cutter directly in line with the extended lines of the pattern.

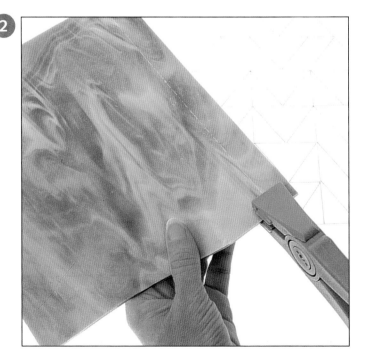

2

2 *Score, then break the piece away with running pliers.*

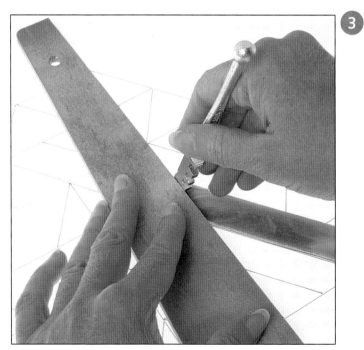

3

3 *Place the strip back on the pattern and trim the end to shape by following the line of the design.*

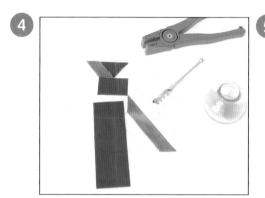

4 *Continue to measure and score the glass in blocks of color, using the geometry of the design as a guide.*

5 *The red is cut into strips then divided into triangles. Break these small pieces apart using the pliers held next to the score in one hand and gripping the glass firmly with the fingers of the other hand.*

6 *Continue cutting to build up the pattern.*

7 *Rub the edges of the glass with the stone, wash and foil the pieces, placing them back on the pattern as you work.*

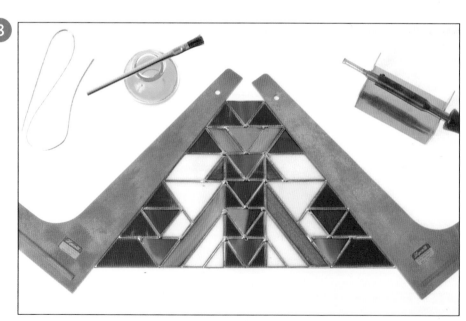

8 *Use two straight edges to keep the sides of the panel straight. This is important as the final assembly will be dependent on the sides being perfectly straight.*

9 *Flux and tack solder the copper seams together, then solder the panel together by fluxing and tinning both sides. Add more solder to one side only and form a beaded seam. The beaded side of the panel will be the outside of the lampshade.*

10 *Each panel should be of exactly the same proportions and identical. Continue to check as you work.*

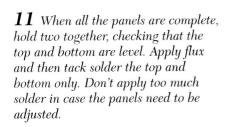

11 *When all the panels are complete, hold two together, checking that the top and bottom are level. Apply flux and then tack solder the top and bottom only. Don't apply too much solder in case the panels need to be adjusted.*

12 *Do the same on the other two panels and when all four panels are tacked into place, tin the seams.*

13 *Turn the shade over and tin the inside seams.*

14 *Lift the shade and support it so that the long seams are as near to a horizontal position as possible. Bead solder along these edges and remember to flux as you go.*

15 *Attach a vase cap by fluxing and soldering it to the four main seams. The vase cap can then be tinned with solder. When all the soldering is complete wash the shade with detergent and hot water to remove flux and oil. Wearing rubber gloves, apply a patina with a sponge and then rinse and wash the shade thoroughly once again.*

These bright and striking pheasants in a golden wheatfield are fabricated using color appliqué with painted detail.

FROEBEL COLLEGE, LONDON

A woodland scene with flamboyant bluebells and foxgloves are created from glass appliqué.

FROEBEL COLLEGE, LONDON

Tiffany Lamp

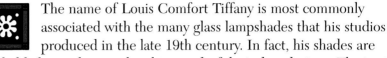

YOU WILL NEED

- ✤ opal glass in white and yellow
- ✤ Uroborus hand cast opal glass for background
- ✤ mold for shade
- ✤ scissors
- ✤ glass cutter
- ✤ grozing pliers
- ✤ carborundum stone
- ✤ ¼ in or ⁷⁄₃₂ copper foil (depending on thickness of glass)
- ✤ fid
- ✤ "tacky wax"
- ✤ solder
- ✤ soldering iron
- ✤ flux and brush
- ✤ patina
- ✤ lamp base

The name of Louis Comfort Tiffany is most commonly associated with the many glass lampshades that his studios produced in the late 19th century. In fact, his shades are probably better known than his wonderful window designs. The intricacy of a curved Tiffany shade fascinates many people, but they are made from small pieces of flat glass assembled over a curved form.

With the aid of pre-patterned commercial molds available to buy, constructing a shade can be a rewarding and surprisingly easy project. There are many designs to choose from and most are copies of Tiffany's originals. Accurate cutting and patience is the key to success.

The kits come with one section or two, depending on the pattern of the complete dome. The design is already printed on the sections as a guide. Included are templates for you to cut out and use as a guide for cutting the glass. As you cannot see through opalescent glass, you will need these templates to lay on the glass for drawing around prior to cutting.

Designs can range from simple to stunningly ornate. Some of the more complex designs can be enhanced with filagrees soldered to the finished shade. These are available from the suppliers along with the molds. Unprinted molds are also available for those who prefer to design their own lampshades.

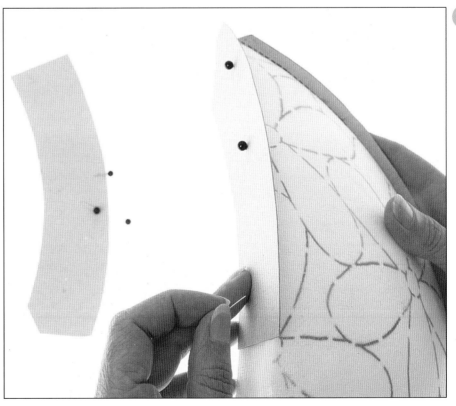

1 *Cardboard "shoulders" are pinned to either side of the mold to keep the pieces of glass in line.*

2 *Cut out the templates carefully and check them against the design on the pattern.*

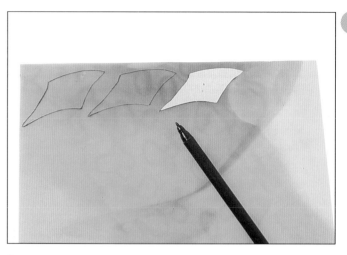

3 *Place the templates on the glass; try to keep the streaks or grain of the glass running in the same direction. Mark around the templates with a felt tip pen or glass crayon.*

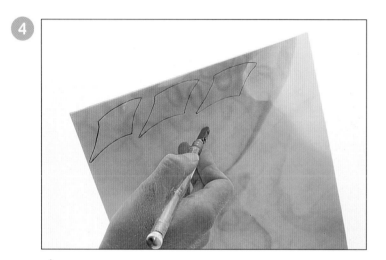

4 *Score and break this strip off before scoring and breaking the individual shapes of glass.*

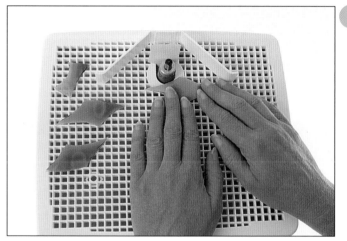

5 *File each piece on a grinding machine or carborundum stone. Wash the pieces in preparation for foiling.*

6 *Now check the pieces of glass against the pattern.*

7 *Copper foil each piece. Place the glass in the center of the foil pressing gently. Check there is an equal amount of foil left on each side and fold this down on to the sides of the glass. Rub down the foiled pieces with a fid or similar instrument.*

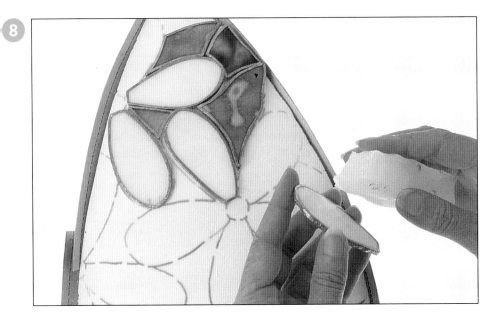

8 *Stick some "tacky wax" behind each piece of glass and assemble all the foiled pieces in their correct places on the form. Press each piece firmly so that they are secure.*

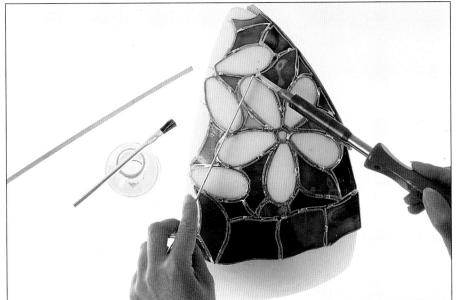

9 *Apply flux and tack solder the pieces together. Continue to flux and solder all the seams. Then bead solder the outer seams. Carefully lift this section off the form.*

10 *Place two interconnecting sections together and tack solder.*

11 *Continue until you have a completed dome.*

12 *Run solder along the joining seams and attach a vase cap to the aperture. Flux and tin the vase cap and join the vase to the shade at the same time via the vertical seams.*

13 *Complete the soldering by beading the seams, attaching the vase cap on the inside of the lamp, and tinning the inside. Wash the lamp well with hot water and detergent to remove all oil and flux residue.*

14 *Apply some patina with a sponge (always wear rubber gloves). Gently rub along all the soldered seams and then repeat the washing process.*

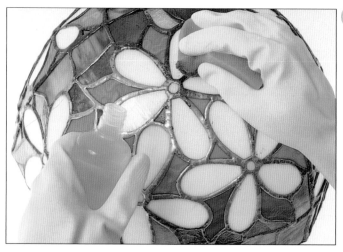

Before most glasswork is undertaken, a drawing or cartoon must be prepared showing the colors of the design and the lines where the glass will be scored and broken. These two rather beautiful cartoons demonstrate this vital first stage.

FROEBEL COLLEGE, LONDON

CHAPTER FIVE

Projects using leading

❖ ❖ ❖

Leading is the traditional technique for making stained glass windows. Strips of lead cames – with a channel down each side to accommodate the glass – are used as the basic skeleton of the window. Not only does the lead hold the pieces of glass together but its linear quality makes it an integral part of the overall design.

Now known as cames and sold in lengths of 6 feet and in a variety of widths, these strips of lead were once more commonly known as "calmes".

Tulip Panel

YOU WILL NEED

+ rolled cathedral glass in 4 colors
+ felt tip pen
+ glass cutter
+ grozing pliers
+ ¼ inch H channel lead came
+ ½ inch H channel lead came
+ horseshoe nails
+ solder
+ soldering iron
+ tallow candle
+ wire wool
+ lead cement
+ whiting powder
+ brush for scrubbing lead
+ fid for opening channels and cleaning lead
+ wooden board and battens
+ grate polish (optional)

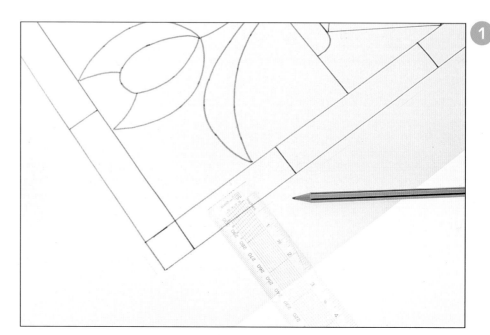

1 *Draw the design, following the pattern on page 149, and make three identical copies. Be sure to draw the lines using a felt tip pen which marks a line the thickness of the heart of the lead. Usually this will be ¹⁄₁₆ inch.*

Measure and draw an extra line of ¼ inch on the inside of the overall measurement. This will indicate the center of the ½ inch lead that will be used on the outside of the panel. Mark in this line with the felt tip pen.

2 *As the glass is so narrow between the tulip and the leaf, you run the risk of it breaking. Make a small mark to indicate where it can be broken*

intentionally. The lead from the tulip and the leaf will touch at this point and cover the break.

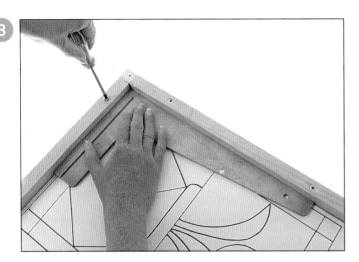

3 Place the pattern on a wooden board and screw or nail down two wooden strips to form right angles. These should be placed next to the external lines on the pattern.

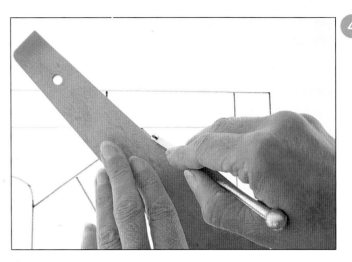

4 Score the glass on the inside of the ¹⁄₁₆ inch lines. Accurate cutting is very important, otherwise the glass will not fit.

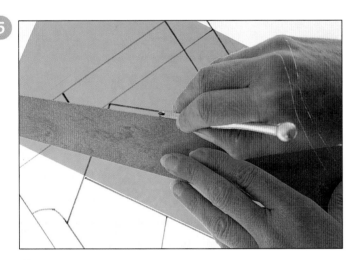

5 Align the cutting wheel with the inside of the line and use the straight edge to score the straight lines.

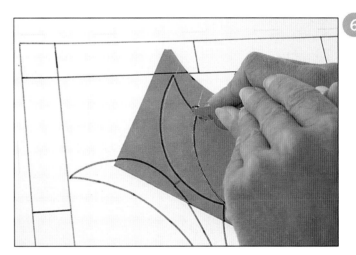

6 Score the curved tulip, taking the vertical lines from one edge of the glass to the other. Return to score the short inner curves.

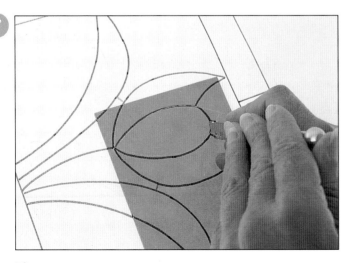

7 Score following the vertical lines first. Then score across the top of the tulip.

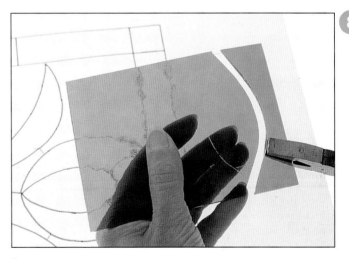

8 Place the edge of the pliers next to the score and support the glass firmly with the other hand. Grip the glass with the pliers and break the score.

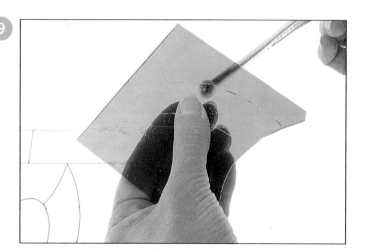

9 *Tap directly underneath the scores with the ball end of the cutter. Remove any sharp points with the pliers by grozing the edges.*

10 *Nibble away any small slivers by gripping them with the pliers and nipping them off.*

11 *Lay all the pieces on to the pattern to check for accuracy. There should be gap of ¹⁄₁₆ inch between each piece of glass.*

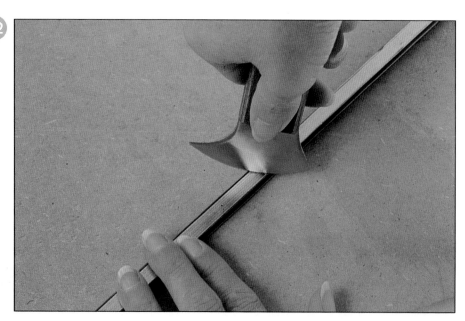

12 *Make sure the lead is stretched prior to use. Cut some lead longer than is required and miter the end with the lead knife. Place the lead knife on top of the lead and press directly downwards, rocking the knife from side to side as you go.*

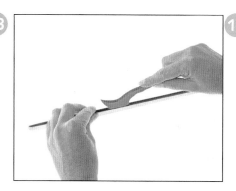

13 *Using the fid, open the lead channel. (If the lead has become flattened, open it with the lead knife.)*

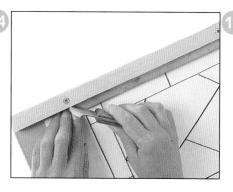

14 *Place the outer lead on the pattern, making sure it fits into the corners. Measure and mark the lead for the next miter.*

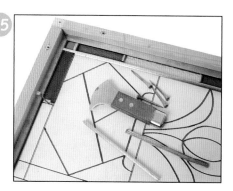

15 *Start from inside the right angle and place the glass in the lead channels. Place the lead and glass alternately. Help the glass to slide in further by tapping it with a small piece of wood placed next to the side of the glass. If the glass has been cut accurately this is not a necessity but where some pieces prove to be a tight fit, a light tap can help.*

16 *Measure and mark the lead with the knife before cutting. Each piece of lead should meet the flange of the adjoining lead and an allowance should be made for the width of the adjoining lead.*

17 *Hold the glass and lead in place as you work with horseshoe nails. Protect the glass by pushing scraps of lead in between the nails and glass.*

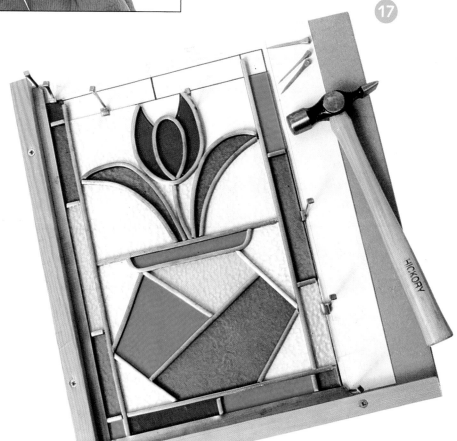

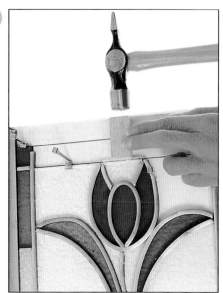

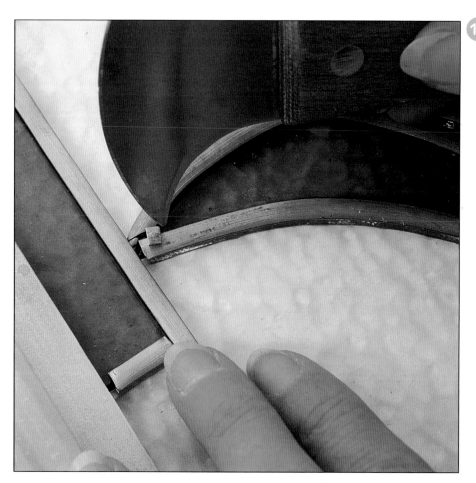

18 *Continue with the pattern, pushing the glass into the channels. (Protect the glass with a piece of wood as you tap it into its place.)*

19 *When the panel has been leaded, inevitably there will be slight gaps between the intersections. These can be filled using slivers of lead packed or pushed into the holes.*

20 *Rub tallow candle flux on to the joints to be soldered.*

21 *Solder at the junctions on both sides. Be careful, as too much heat can cause the came itself to melt. Lift the iron off almost as soon as it has made contact with the lead.*

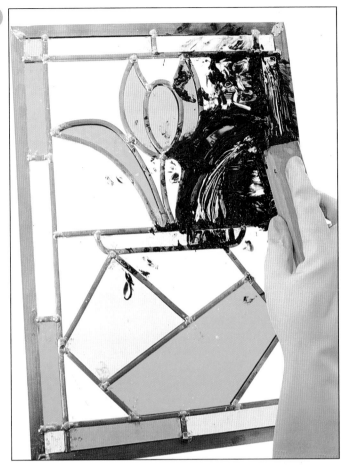

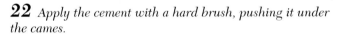

22 *Apply the cement with a hard brush, pushing it under the cames.*

23 *Scatter whiting over the panel. Allow the cement to partly dry, then remove the excess cement from around the cames with a fid.*

24 *Brush the panel vigorously. The whiting will absorb the oil from the cement and clean the glass. The leads will darken slowly as you continue to brush. To darken the cames further apply some grate polish. Turn over and repeat the process.*

A Victorian painted roundel depicts a robin on a bramble stem. Set into a traditional leaded panel, it is an excellent example of early domestic stained glass.

Deep sandblasting produces a three-dimensional quality in this beautiful leaded panel.

RHIANNON MORGAN

Leaded Light Window

YOU WILL NEED

- ✤ clear water glass for background
- ✤ colored glue and yellow chip glass for border
- ✤ felt tip pen
- ✤ glass cutter
- ✤ grozing pliers
- ✤ ¼ inch H channel lead came
- ✤ ½ inch H channel lead came
- ✤ solder
- ✤ soldering iron
- ✤ tallow candle
- ✤ wire wool
- ✤ lead cement
- ✤ whiting powder
- ✤ brush for scrubbing lead
- ✤ fid for opening channels and cleaning lead
- ✤ wooden board and battens
- ✤ grate polish (optional)

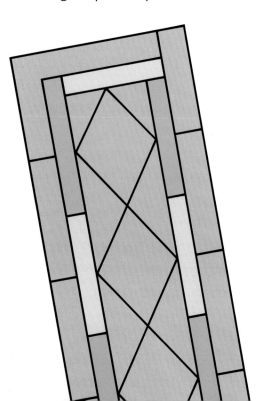

 This window panel has been made to fit into a specific door frame. The same simple design could be adapted to fit any other door or window frame.

Take care to protect the panel when fitting it back into the frame. Careless hammering of the beading could crack the glass.

1 *Take out the beading or scrape out the putty from the rebate of the door or window and measure the opening for the width and height. Subtract ¹⁄₁₆ inch from the height and the width and then draw out the cartoon (see page 150). (Subtracting this from the overall measurement will give some room for the window to be comfortably "fitted" into the opening of the door.)*

Make two copies of the original cartoon. Draw all the lines with a felt tip pen the width of the central channel of the lead. Make an additional line ¼ inch from the inside of the external measurement. As the outer piece of lead is to be ½ inch in width, this additional line will indicate where to cut the glass that will fit into this lead.

Lay the pattern on to a large board and nail down battens at right angles in one corner, next to the outer lines of the design. (The battens should extend beyond the length of the vertical and horizontal outer lines.)

Cut out all the glass, leaving the ¹⁄₁₆ inch gap for the lead between each

piece. Measure and cut two strips of the ½ inch lead and lay them on the inside of the battens. Measure to the required length on the pattern and miter or butt joint the ends.

2 *Start placing or slotting the pieces of cut glass into the channels of the lead, separating each of the pieces with another piece of ¼ inch lead. Take care to measure each piece and make an allowance for the next strip of lead that will lay alongside.*

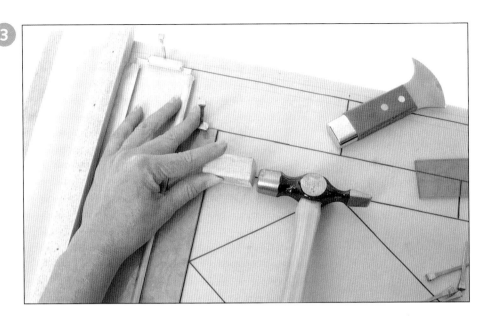

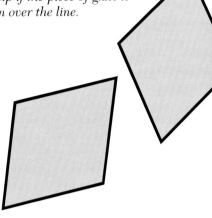

3 A gentle tap with a piece of wood will help the glass sink into the lead heart. This is not always necessary, but it may help if the piece of glass is just a fraction over the line.

4 Place the glass and lead alternately. Measure and cut the lead to allow space for the corresponding strip.

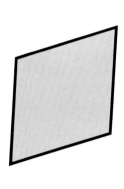

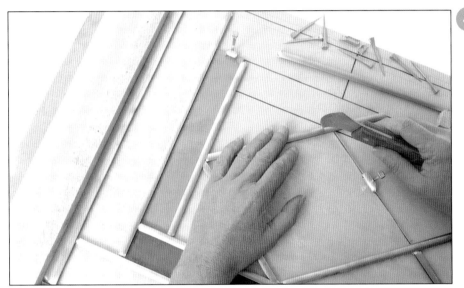

5 When the panel is complete, rub tallow flux on to the intersections. If the lead has oxidized, rub each intersection first with a little wire wool or wire brush. Melt only enough solder at each junction to cover and join where the lead cames meet.

6 After the panel has been soldered at the junctions on both sides, brush cement into the gaps between the glass and the cames. Turn the panel over and repeat the cementing. This process will strengthen and weatherproof the panel.

7 Sprinkle some whiting on to the glass and cames. This will help to absorb the oil from the cementing and also clean the glass.

8 *Allow the cement to party dry. Use a fid or wooden stick to remove excess cement from the cames.*

9 *Brush the panel vigorously to remove excess cement and powder from the glass and the cames. The cames will darken with continued brushing but adding some black grate polish will help to darken the cames further.*

10 *Sit the lower section of the glass into the opening of the frame and against the rebate. Carefully push the window back to rest against the rest of the rebate.*

11 *If the window does not fit easily, or is slightly out of line, trim the external lead with a sharp lead knife. Just removing a sliver of lead may be all that's required to allow the window to fit. Replace the beading or putty the glass in place.*

The versatility of glasswork is amply demonstrated in this wonderful appliqué window featuring little birds, foliage and a bright blue sky.

FROEBEL COLLEGE, LONDON

CHAPTER SIX

Projects using appliqué

❖ ❖ ❖

The application of glass on to glass is a straightforward technique that does not involve lead or copper foil. A panel or window is created either by using left-over scraps of glass, or glass cut to a specified design. The pieces are then glued to a panel of ⅛ or ¼ inch clear glass. Black or gray "grout" is used to fill the areas in between the glass. This technique offers a great deal of freedom and creativity.

Vase of Flowers

YOU WILL NEED

- ✤ ⅛ inch clear glass (cut to required size of panel)
- ✤ assortment of colored glass pieces
- ✤ felt tip pen
- ✤ glass pliers
- ✤ grozing pliers
- ✤ carborundum stone
- ✤ silicone adhesive
- ✤ universal stainer
- ✤ interior plaster filler

1 *Consider the glass you have available and if necessary cut some into specific shapes. For example, the* tulip *was cut following a small sketch while the glass stems were formed from existing pieces.*

2 *Cut the vase from the largest piece of glass available.*

3 *Lay the pieces on to plain glass cut to size. Use sticky pads or adhesive putty to fasten down the glass as you work, cutting or selecting pieces the appropriate size or color.*

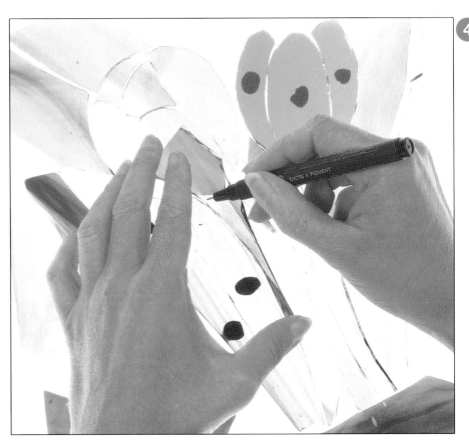

4 *To fill in gaps between pieces you can lay glass over the shape and mark it with a felt tip pen prior to cutting.*

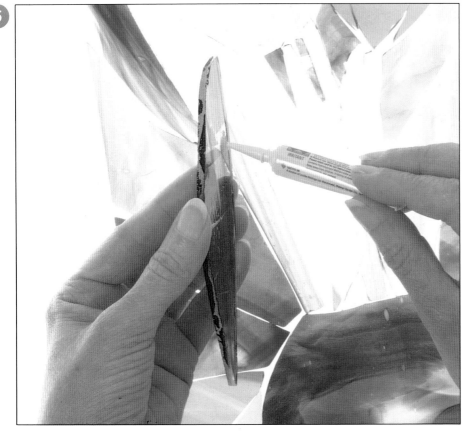

5 *Apply adhesive to the back of each piece and press it firmly on to the glass. Allow to dry thoroughly. Take* *care to cover the glass completely with the glue to prevent the filler from seeping underneath.*

6 *Mix black universal stain into some interior filler then add water. Keep the consistency thick.*

7 *Fill the gaps between the glass with this mixture.*

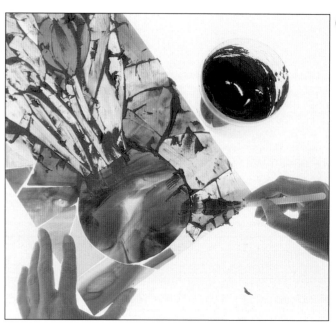

8 *Work your way down the panel "grouting" the glass.*

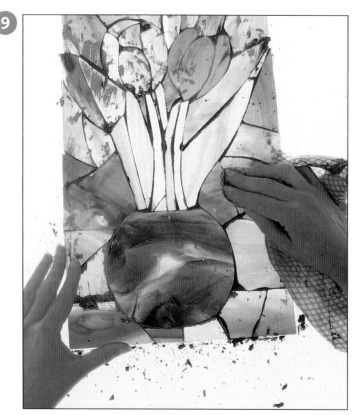

9 *Allow the mixture to dry, then wipe away the excess from the surface.*

10 *Rub the surface of the grout with wire wool to smooth it. If desired, this whole process can be repeated again to raise the surface of the grout with the level of the glass.*

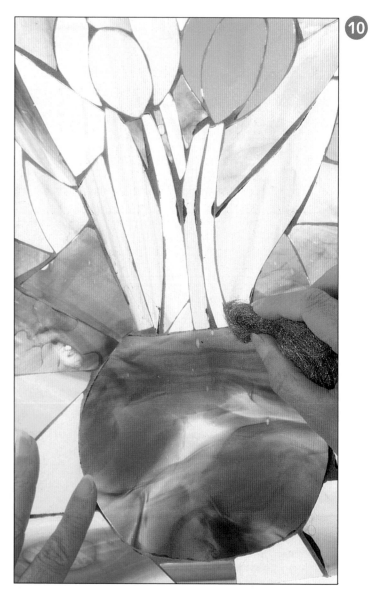

These stunning leaded panels have been decorated using deep sandblasting and acid polishing.

RHIANNON MORGAN

CHAPTER SEVEN

Projects using sandblasting

Sandblasting is the technique of removing or abraiding a glass surface. The process of sandblasting is not far removed from spray painting except color is removed rather than added from flashed or mirrored glass. It will create an etched surface giving a frosted appearance on transparent or clear colored glass.

Frosted Vase

YOU WILL NEED

- ✤ clear glass vase
- ✤ vinyl resist
- ✤ paper and pencil
- ✤ scalpel
- ✤ felt tip pen

1 Cut a piece of resist, large enough to surround the vase. Clean the vase thoroughly and, pulling back a corner of the film, stick down the adhesive film on to the glass. Rub the film smooth and try to avoid air bubbles forming underneath.

2 Slowly continue to pull back the protective paper, smoothing the film down on to the vase.

3 *Draw the design on to paper and place this inside the vase. Trace the design through the glass and on to the film with a felt tip pen.*

4 *With a scalpel knife cut around the outline of the pattern.*

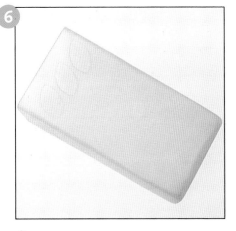

5 *Cut and remove the surrounding resist, taking care not to lift off the area of resist on the design. Spend a few moments rubbing the edges of the design so they are firmly in contact with the glass. The force of the sandblaster could lift these pieces if they are not secure.*

6 *Put the prepared vase in the sandblasting machine and hold with one hand while you blast with the other. When finished, rinse with water.*

7 *Remove the pieces of resist with the scalpel and rinse again to remove any glass dust.*

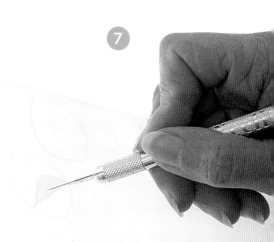

Large and small pieces of antique glass are used effectively in this splendid glass appliqué window.

FROEBEL COLLEGE, LONDON

Leaf in the Fall

YOU WILL NEED

✤ red on yellow French flashed glass

✤ straight edge

✤ glass cutter

✤ grozing pliers

✤ vinyl resist

✤ paper and pencil

✤ felt tip pen

✤ scalpel

✤ orange stick

✤ wood adhesive

✤ brass strip for edging

✤ flux and brush

✤ solder and soldering iron

✤ brass wire for hanging

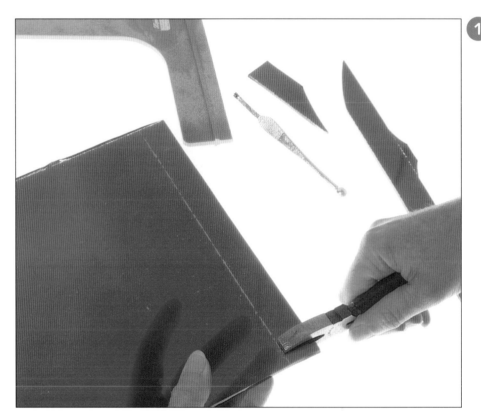

1 Following the pattern on page 152, use the straight edge to score the straight lines. Break the glass to the size indicated on the pattern.

2 If the break is not completely successful, use the pliers to "nip" off irregular edges.

3 Cut a piece of resist larger than the size of the glass.

4 Peel back a small section of the protective paper and lay the resist on to the flashed side of the glass.

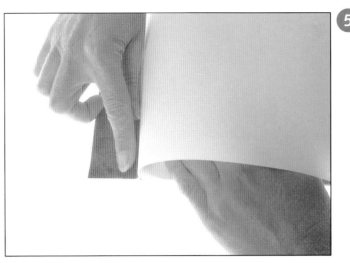

5 As you pull back the paper about an inch at a time, smooth the film down to make firm contact with the glass. Moving too quickly can cause air bubbles.

6 Trace the design on the pattern through the glass with a felt tip pen.

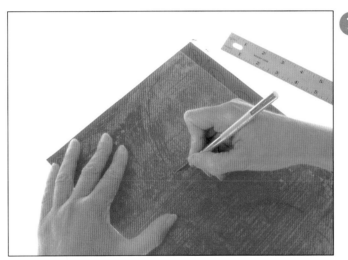

7 Carefully score the outline of the leaf.

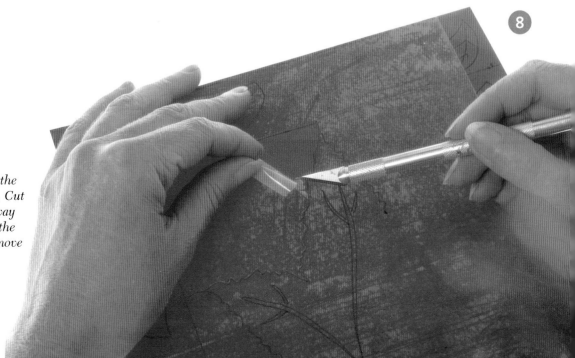

8 Remove the film from around the leaf but leave the border covered. Cut and pull thin strips of the film away on the inside of the leaf. Cut out the oval leaves on the border and remove the film from these shapes only.

9 *With the orange stick, apply thin lines of detail with wood adhesive on the exposed red glass. Allow to dry. Place the panel into the sandblasting unit with the resist side of the glass facing you. Close the door. The sand jet should be sprayed across the glass surface in a continuous sweeping motion. Depending upon the pressure and the type of abrasive sand (we recommend 49psi with a fine grit), the red flash glass will be removed quickly. Start from the top and work downward taking care to keep the jet*

moving constantly. Notice how a shading effect can be achieved as the sand removes the flash. When all of the red has been removed, stop blasting and remove the panel from the unit. Peel off all the resist and wash the panel carefully.

10 *Miter some brass edging to fit around the panel.*

11 *Flux and solder the corners and add two loops of brass wire at each corner for hanging.*

Graceful flamingoes form these leaded front door windows and coordinating panel above.

MATHEW LLOYD WINDER

Leaded and painted window panels commissioned by a literary agent to commemorate her involvement with publishing. Note the graphic use of paint on the leaves and figures.

MATHEW LLOYD WINDER

ABOVE: *Two of these panels have been restored to match the originals. They incorporate painted, stained and enameled roses.*

ABOVE: *Stained glass has won a place in many homes. These traditional door and window panels were popular in houses of the 1920s and 1930s.*

An excellent example of early domestic stained glass. This leaded and painted Victorian roundel shows craftsmen at work. Note the rich fruit and leaf border.

Shell Mirror

YOU WILL NEED

- ⅛ inch mirrored glass
- glass cutter
- grozing pliers
- paper, pencil and ruler
- scissors
- scalpel
- vinyl resist
- felt tip pen
- wet and dry sandpaper
- small square block of wood with D ring screwed on
- strong adhesive

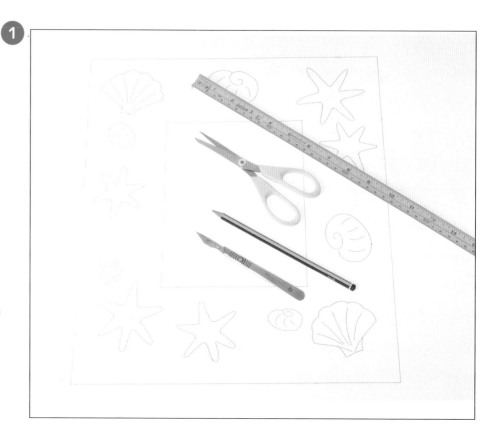

1 Measure and draw the pattern on page 153 to size. Cut the mirror to size.

2 Slowly peel back the protective paper from the resist and apply it to the edge of the mirror. Carefully rub down the adhesive film as you peel back the paper inch by inch.

3 Cut the rectangle from the pattern and center it on the resist covered mirror.

4 *Mark around it with a felt-tip pen.*

5 *Cut out the motif from the pattern, arrange them on the border and mark around them with a pen.*

6 *With a scalpel cut around these shapes. Leave the resist on the rectangle and on the shells and starfish. These will remain reflective.*

7 *Copy the detail freehand on to the shells.*

8 *Make sure the resist is firmly in contact with the mirror backing and carefully rub down the resist, especially on the edges.*

Prop the mirror into the sandblasting machine with the resist and mirror backing facing you. Close the door and turn on the compressor and extractor. Using pressure of no more than 40psi, blast the exposed areas, moving the nozzle from left to right and from top to bottom. Blast until all the mirror backing has been removed.

Wash off the sand from the mirror and use the wet and dry sandpaper to smooth the edges. Allow to dry before screwing a picture hook or D ring on to a 3 inch-square piece of wood and glue this to the back for hanging..

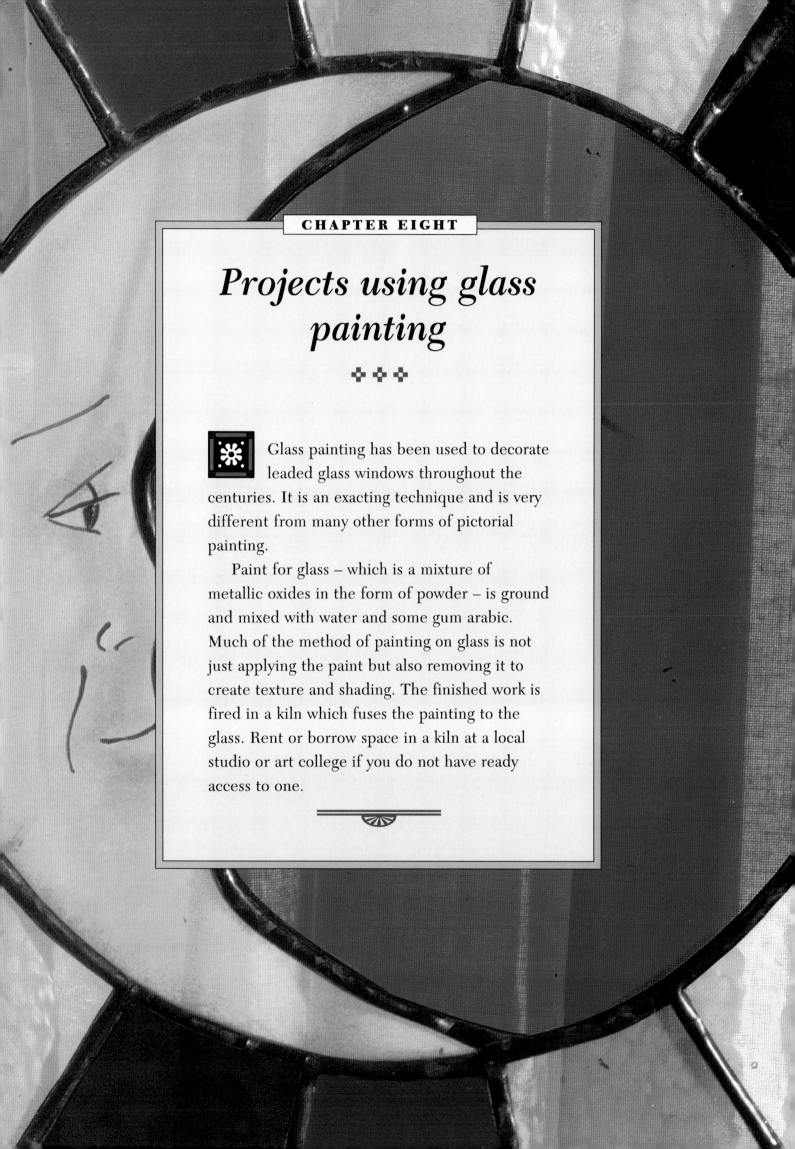

CHAPTER EIGHT

Projects using glass painting

❖ ❖ ❖

Glass painting has been used to decorate leaded glass windows throughout the centuries. It is an exacting technique and is very different from many other forms of pictorial painting.

Paint for glass – which is a mixture of metallic oxides in the form of powder – is ground and mixed with water and some gum arabic. Much of the method of painting on glass is not just applying the paint but also removing it to create texture and shading. The finished work is fired in a kiln which fuses the painting to the glass. Rent or borrow space in a kiln at a local studio or art college if you do not have ready access to one.

Pear Panel

YOU WILL NEED

+ Polish antique clear and dark green glass

FOR PAINTING:

+ black trace paint

+ gum arabic

+ palette knife

+ scrap of glass to serve as palette

+ trace brush

+ shade paint for matting

+ mop brush

+ badger brush

+ stipple brush

+ short stiff paintbrush

+ silver stain

+ washing-up sponge with abrasive side

FOR LEADING:

+ glass cutter

+ grozing pliers

+ horseshoe nails

+ U section lead

+ H section lead

+ tallow candle

+ solder

+ soldering iron

 This project combines painted glass with leading. I made it with a U lead border as it has been designed as a piece to hang. It is not cemented as other leaded projects because it is not to be used externally. However, there's no reason why it could not be adopted for a window panel if you wish.

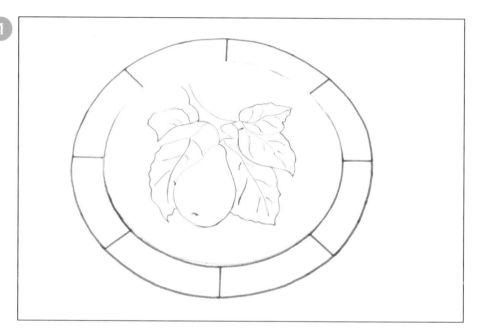

1 *Clean the piece of clear antique glass and place directly over the* *pattern (taken from page 154) in preparation for painting.*

2 *Mix the trace paint thoroughly after adding a few drops of water to* *obtain a thick creamy consistency. Add only a few drops at a time.*

3

3 *Mix and grind the paint well with the palette knife. Add a drop of gum arabic. Mix again and add some more water to obtain a workable consistency. Test the mixture on a separate piece of glass with a brush to check its density.*

4

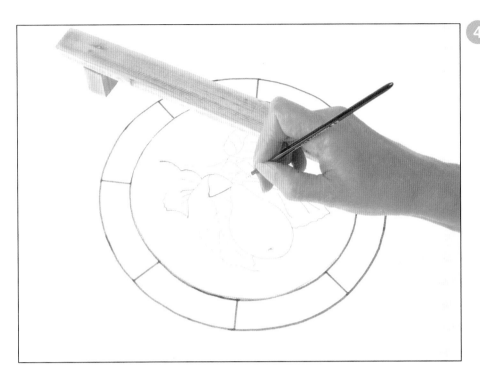

5

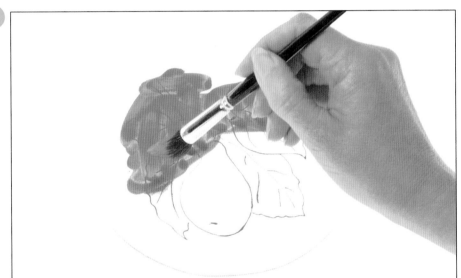

6

4 *Load the trace brush with paint and, while resting your arm on a rest, make one continuous stroke with the brush. This may require some practice to start with, but if you make a mistake the paint can be wiped off (but this must be done thoroughly) and you can begin again. Remember never to re-touch a stroke or go over a painted line with another, as the paint will blister in the kiln. Each sweep with the brush must be a single movement. Re-load the brush and begin the next line just where the previous one ended.*

   When the tracing is complete, fire the piece at a temperature of 1250°F. Care should be taken when removing the glass from the kiln as there is a danger of the piece cracking with a sudden change of temperature. Allow the piece to rest in the kiln after firing is complete until the temperature has dropped below 395°F. Electric kilns generally have annealing chambers for this purpose.

5 *Mix the shade paint in the same way as the trace paint and apply with sweeps of the mop brush.*

6 *Move the paint over the glass in different directions using the badger brush, be sure to maintain a consistent layer on the surface.*

7 *After the paint has dried, use the stipple brush to dab the paint and create a texture on the surface. Stipple a little more in some areas to achieve lighter tones.*

8 *With the end of a paintbrush or a stick, define the outline. Remove the excess paint with a short stiff paintbrush. Fire the piece once again at approximately 1250°F. (This will vary with different kilns.)*

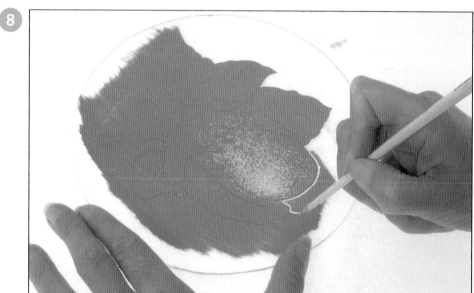

9 *Now mix the silver stain, but it is not necessary to add gum arabic. Apply it to the back of the glass with a mop brush (keep stain brushes separate from shading brushes) and then "sweep" it with light, even strokes in different directions with the badger brush, maintaining a consistent layer. Remove excess paint from around the pear as you would for shade color. Fire the piece at a approximately 1110°F. When it has been fired and cooled, remove the residue on the back of the glass by washing with the abrasive side of the washing-up sponge.*

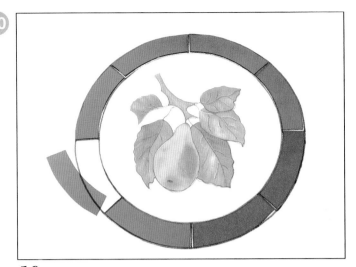

10 *Cut the glass pieces surrounding the painted section and assemble them.*

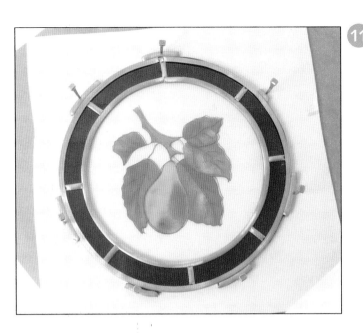

11 *Surround the painted disc in lead first and then add the intersected lead and glass border. The exterior lead is pinned in place with horseshoe nails. Place scrap lead in between the exterior lead and the nails for protection.*

12 *Apply tallow wax to the intersecting joints.*

13 *Now solder the joints. Turn the disc over and apply the wax and solder.*

incorporate
exquisitely painted
Victorian glass
fragments into the
design.

LEO AMERY

Painted Moon

YOU WILL NEED

GLASS FOR BORDER:

✤ various colors of rolled cathedral and dark blue flash

✤ blue antique glass for background

✤ yellow antique glass for moon

✤ glass cutter

✤ grozing pliers

✤ carborundum stone

✤ ⁷⁄₃₂ copper foil

✤ solder and soldering iron

✤ flux and flux brush

✤ copper sulphate

✤ picture wire for hanging

FOR PAINTING:

✤ trace paint

✤ shading color

✤ gum arabic

✤ glass palette

✤ palette knife

✤ trace brush

✤ mop brush

✤ badger brush

✤ short-bristle hoghair brush

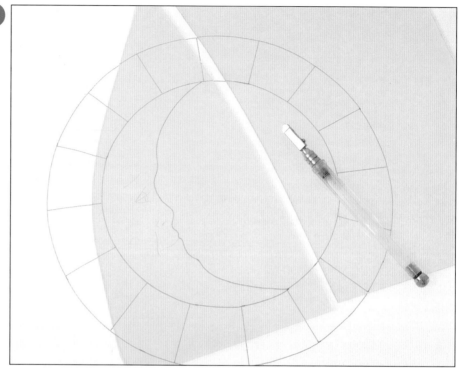

1 *For the moon, score and break a section of glass to a suitable size. Make at least two copies of the pattern on page 155.*

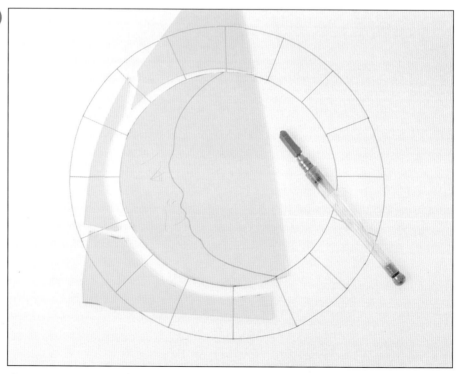

2 *Following the pattern, score the outside curve first and break.*

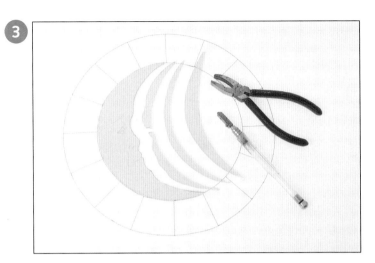

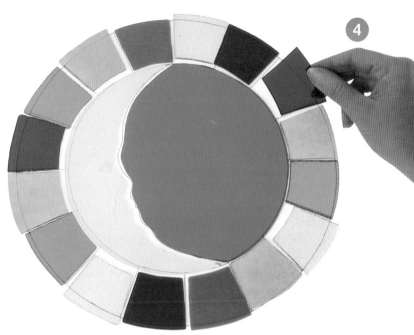

3 *Score the inside following the curves of the face. Make a series of scores next to each other and with the pliers, break each one. Hold the pliers next to the score each time. Hold the glass firmly with the other hand. If there is too much resistance when you try to pull out the glass, use the end of a cutter to tap the score from underneath until you see a change in the appearance of the score. Use the pliers to ease the glass out.*

4 *Cut out the border from a selection of colors. Check all the pieces fit well on the pattern. Two pieces of the glass we have chosen are flashed and will be sandblasted (see step 8).*

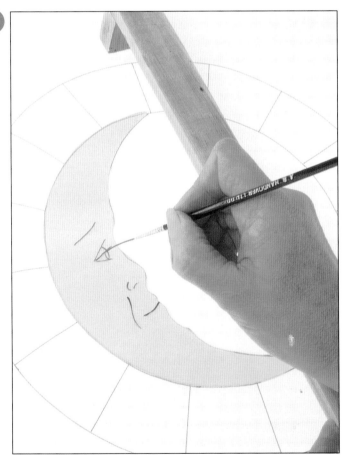

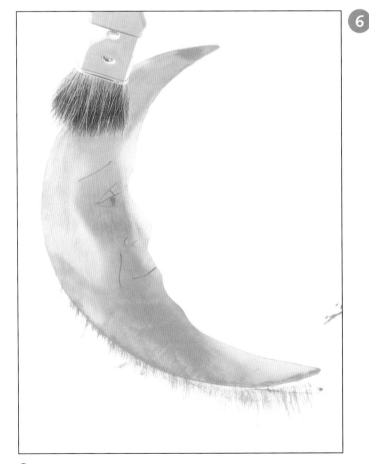

5 *To paint the face of the moon, first mix the trace paint and then apply as step 00, page 00. With the arm on a rest to steady the hand, make one continual stroke with the trace brush for each line on the face. Fire the moon in the kiln at approximately 1250°F.*

6 *Mix the shade color and after applying with a mop brush make some criss-cross or diagonal strokes with the badger to distribute the paint evenly.*

7 *We used a short bristle hoghair paintbrush to stipple the shade color to tone and contour the face. The moon is fired once again at the same temperature.*

8 *Cover the pieces of blue glass in the border with resist and cut out small star shapes to expose the flashed glass ready for sandblasting. (This technique is optional to the project but is described in the chapter on sandblasting.)*

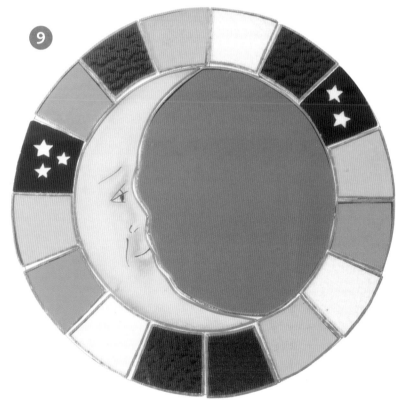

9 *Carefully rub the edges of all the pieces with the stone, then wash and foil them.*

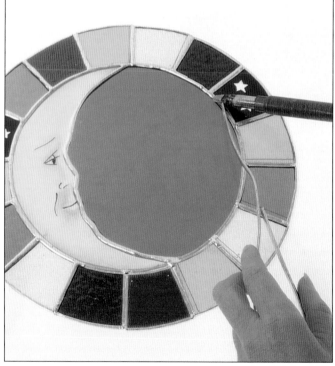

10 *Flux and tack solder the pieces in place. Flux once again and tin solder the whole project both front and back. On the front side only, bead the seam with more solder. To hang the project, two short pieces of copper or brass picture wire can be formed into loops and soldered into the seams. Always solder these into the vertical seam and not just along the top or outside edge of the foil, as they will not hold the weight of the item Finish with the copper sulphate patina and wash thoroughly.*

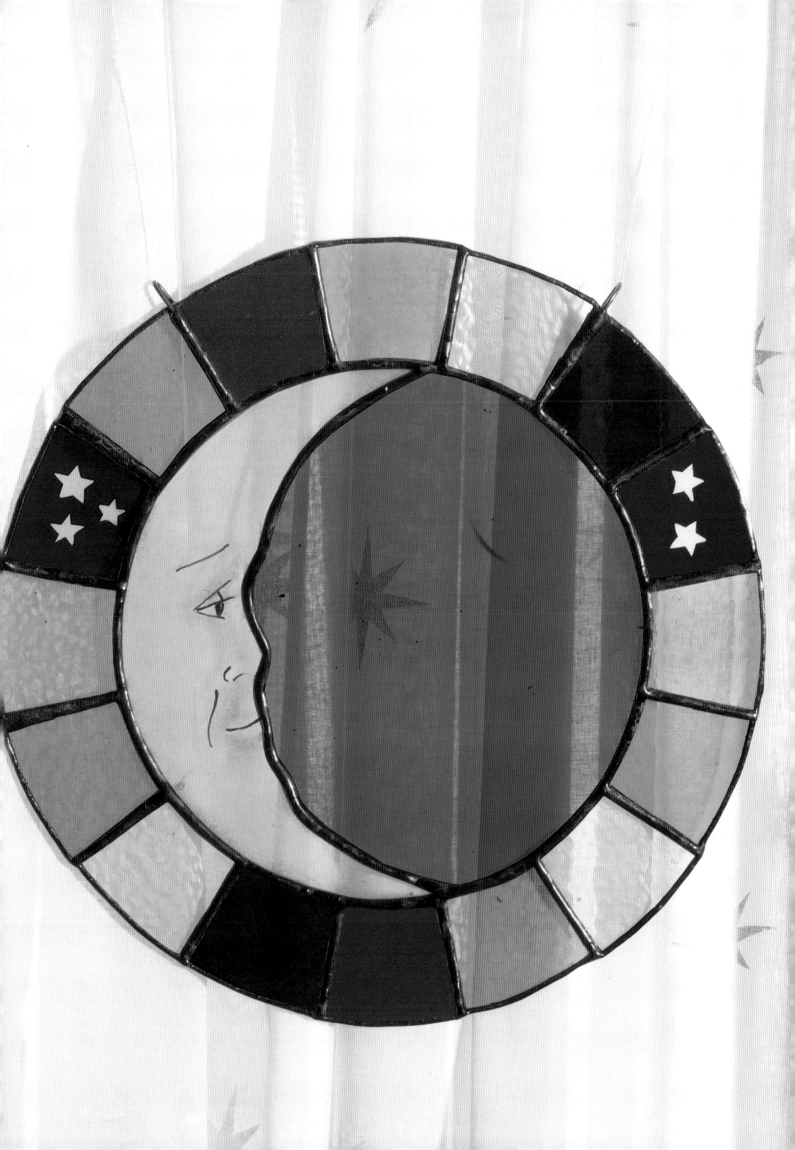

Stunning examples of glass appliqué.
FROEBEL COLLEGE

CHAPTER NINE

Turning a hobby into a business

❖ ❖ ❖

 Working with stained glass purely for your own satisfaction is very different from that made for the commercial world.

The jump from working with glass as a creative hobby to applying your abilities and talents to please paying customers is not insignificant. The marketplace where people compare and reject work can be a difficult reality for some craftspeople to accept. Working in glass for re-sale carries an entirely new range of considerations and before renting a studio and hanging out a sign it is helpful to consider the paths available.

 The home of any proficient glass artist will eventually have all the window panels and lampshades it can comfortably absorb and you will have either to move house or seek new locations where your art can be displayed. Of course, you can continue by giving away your work to friends and relatives, but this too has a limit, especially as the expense of your hobby adds up.

There are two types of glassworker today in the marketplace. The "product" worker is the individual who has decided to develop a specific range or type of glasswork which he or she will repeat again and again. Books and more books abound giving ideas for lampshades, window ornaments and candle holders, and this "product" market is crowded. The best place to start is by selling directly to your customers via a craft market where the immediate feedback, low costs and direct payment for the full value of your work is a tremendous advantage. The alternative is developing a product that can be marked-up by at least 50 per cent for retailers to sell on. Everyone who works with glass soon realizes that the high labor content makes profitability difficult when producing on a small scale. Try to develop work that is unique or unusual in some way and avoid competing head on with the large manufacturers.

COMMISSION WORK

The opportunities of creating one-off pieces can be both an exciting and frustrating experience. Most glass craftspeople will offer a ready-made product which they will sell through a shop or market, and inform potential customers that they are very willing to take on commission work. Getting started on a successful commission means first establishing what the client requires, second, if it is feasible and third the cost. Most people starting out will not have enough of their own work to photograph to fill a portfolio. However, there are many books that are available to illustrate the different styles that you can produce confidently. Use these in addition to photographs or drawings of your own. Some clients know exactly what they require but most will want to consider several alternatives before settling on a particular design.

Once the three basics have been positively established and the details concerning fitting and delivery have been discussed, request a cash deposit before making any preliminary drawings. A deposit changes a casual inquiry into a binding agreement and gives both the artist and the client a firm footing to work through the next stages. How much preliminary drawing you are prepared to do is usually a matter of experience and the originality of the work. Windows commissioned from existing photographs or patterns are simply a matter of scaling up to size and adapting. Original work can involve a lengthy process of design and evaluation.

Show your client different examples of glass and a design that is accepted before you begin work. Allowing a client to inspect work in progress is usually an invitation for making alterations. Remember, they have shown confidence that you are capable of creating a piece in the first place and now it is up to you to complete it.

PRICING WORK

The thrill of realizing that people are actually willing to pay for the object you have made should not be compensation in itself. There can be no denying the pleasure of a total stranger carefully appraising your work and making the decision to buy it. Even after running a commercial studio for more than 20 years, there is still a certain tingle of pleasure when a contract is signed or a small window ornament is purchased. The idea of creating something by hand and being paid for it is a concept that seems too good to be true. Over the years we have met many talented glass artists who almost display a sense of guilt when the topic of value and pricing their work is mentioned.

Like any business, the selling price of your work should be carefully worked out to equal the true cost plus that elusive element known as profit. Although by no means a complete guide to a pricing strategy, some of the basic principles we apply to our work before the price tag can be considered are as follows.

The easy part of pricing is the simple calculation of the value of the materials used. However, as glasswork is a labor-intensive craft, the actual time taken to complete any piece can be the most important element to consider. Like the glass itself, time has a value which is proportional to ability and experience. It's always easier to undervalue your labor and sell your work at a lower price, but is it realistic? In the long term selling your time too cheaply will undermine the quality of your work. Does the estimated cost of materials plus your time equal the price you seek? It seems so obvious but, so often, craftworkers neglect to add on the basic cost of running their business when estimating their work. Unless you live in a tent with no electricity or water and were given your tools, worktable etc, you should add a certain percentage to every commission or product to cover these overheads. Craftspeople who fail to recognize all these costs will find themselves busily turning materials into work with little to show for their effort except the satisfaction of the work itself.

When pricing commissions, we recommend that you record all the information first and then submit your estimate after you have had the opportunity to evaluate carefully what is required. The desire to price a job too quickly will often lead to under-pricing. A difficult or unusual design that perhaps you have not attempted before? Separating the cost of the drawing from the work itself will give both you and your client a clear idea of how much time you are able to allocate to each stage. After you have completed quite a few commissions you will be able to work out costs by comparisons. For windows we are comfortable working on a variable rate per square foot depending upon the complexity of the design, total area and type of glass.

 On the following pages, we have reproduced accurate patterns of the projects featured on pages 64 to 139. Enlarge the chosen pattern on a photocopier using the percentage enlargement provided. Obviously, you can adjust these depending on your own individual requirements.

ENLARGE BY 200%

ENLARGE BY 200%

ENLARGE BY 125%

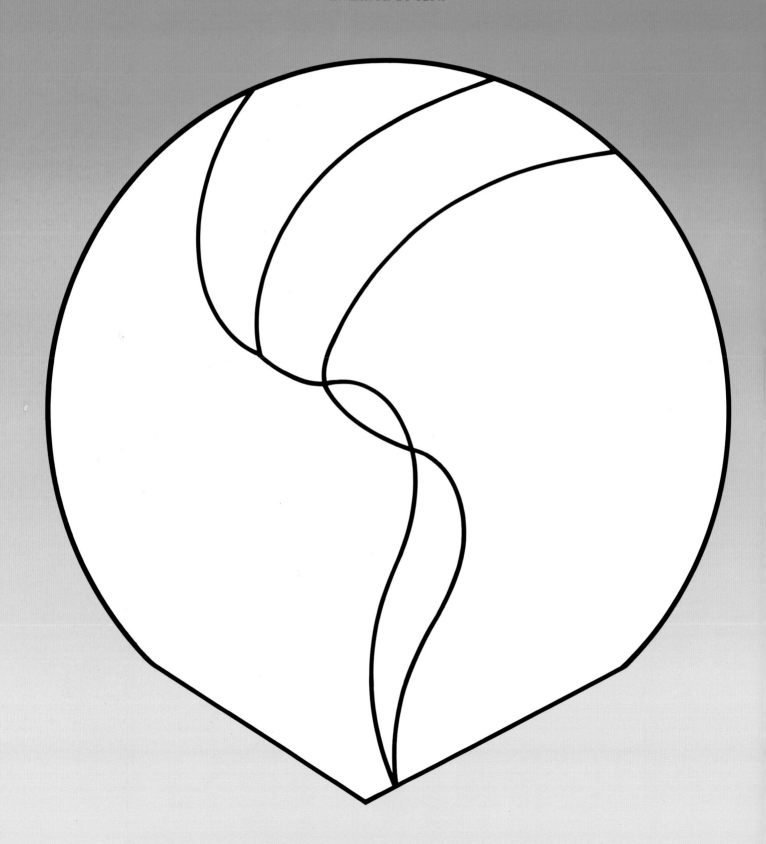

ENLARGE BY 150%

The Tiffany-style lampshade which appears on page 89, is one of a wide selection of kits available from specialist stained glass suppliers. Here, we feature just four other traditional designs available.

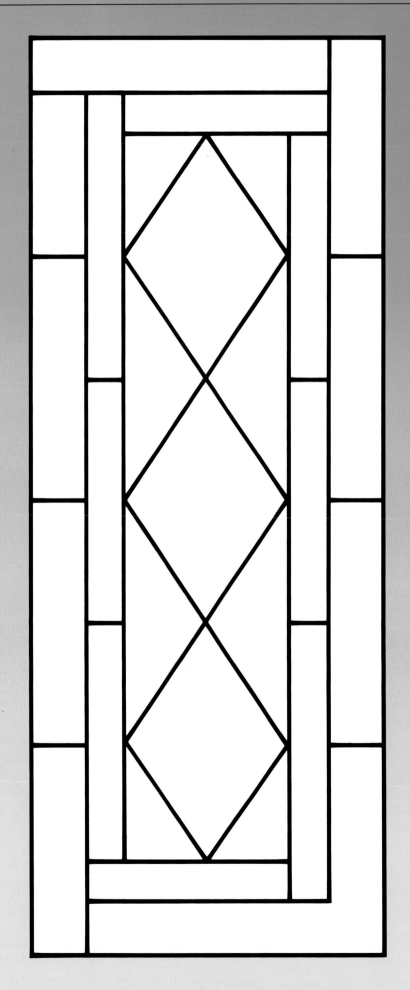

Enlarge to fit your window.

Here, we feature five various designs that are easy to trace and cut from the vinyl resist to apply to your vase ready for sandblasting. Simple shapes, such as these, generally work better than complex shapes for newcomers to this technique.

ENLARGE BY 200%

ENLARGE BY 130%

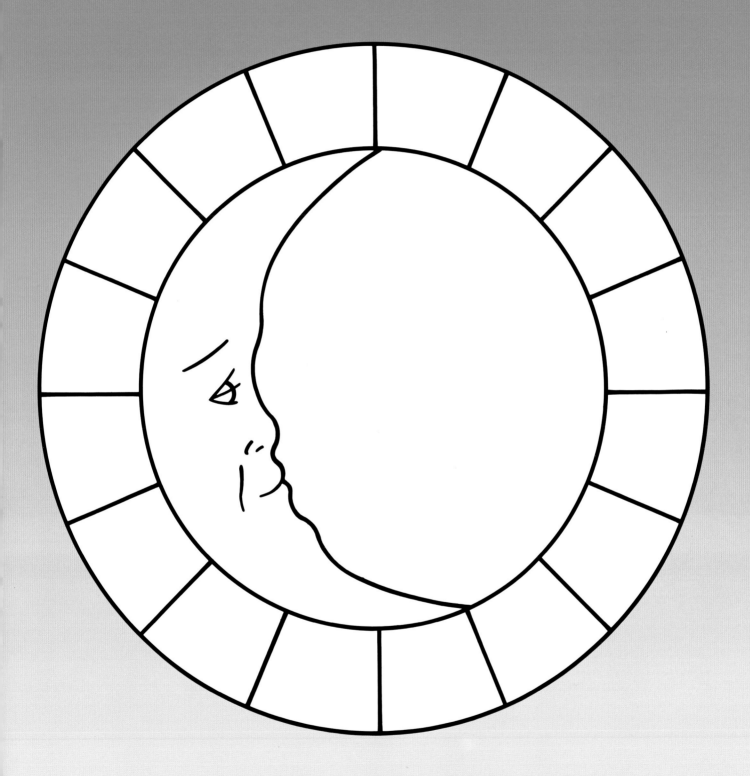

ENLARGE BY 160%

Glossary

ANTIQUE GLASS: A term refering to mouth blown flat glass. It is not as its name implies – "aged" or old. Colors range from deep rich tones to pale tints and each piece may be different with striations and texture and non uniform in thickness. Within this category you will also find plain, seedy, streaky, reamy and flashed antique.

BEADING: Melting enough solder to form a "bead" or rounded seam over copper foil.

BEVELS: Shapes of glass with angles ground into the edges and polished.

BREAKING PLIERS: An aid to breaking glass along the score line.

CARBORUNDUM STONE: A hand tool for sanding or smoothing the edges of glass.

CARTOON: The working drawing or design of a window showing all the lead widths and cut lines to be followed. Several copies of this "original" would be made.

CATHEDRAL GLASS: A machine-made transparent glass.

CEMENTING: The process of forcing lead light cement into gaps between the lead and glass leaving the panel watertight and strong.

COPPER FOIL: A variety of different widths of copper foil with an adhesive backing applied to pieces of glass for bonding together. Commonly used in lampshades and internal or intricate window panels and useful for sculptural or three dimensional objects.

CUT LINE: The line marked on the cartoon depicting where to cut the glass.

CUTTING SQUARE: Specialized ruler used as a guide for cutting right angles.

ETCHING: Applying hydrofluoric acid to the surface of the glass either to remove the top layer of flashed glass or as a decorative technique on clear glass.

FID: Plastic multi-purpose instrument used for opening lead cames and rubbing down copper foil on to the glass.

FIRING: A process requiring a kiln into which glass that has been painted is "fired".

FLASHED GLASS: A glass of one color that has a thin layer of another color on top. The base glass can either be clear (white) or colored. The surface color can be etched or sandblasted away to reveal the base glass.

FLUX: A chemical that allows solder to flow on to the surface of the metals to be joined.

FLUXING: Applying a liquid flux to copper foil before soldering.

FUSING: The art of melting one glass directly on to another in a kiln.

FOILING: The process of wrapping copper foil around the edges of glass.

GLASS CUTTER: A hand tool used for scoring glass.

GLASS NUGGETS: Irregular rounded pieces of thick colored glass in various colors and sizes.

GRINDING MACHINE: Electrically powered machine with a rotating wheel to grind pieces of glass into shapes.

GROZING: The method of removing fine shards and slivers from the edges of a piece of glass.

GROZING PLIERS: Pliers with a narrow head and fine teeth for grozing glass.

HORSESHOE NAILS: Flat sided nails used to stabilize the lead cames during the leading process.

KILN: A specialized oven made of firebrick powered by gas or electricity.

LAMINATED GLASS: Two layers of glass bonded together by a resin.

LATHE: Used to open the lead channels.

LEAD CAME: Lengths of lead with channels on either side to accommodate glass. Used mainly for windows and more durable than copper foil. Available in many different widths.

LEAD STRETCHER: A specialized vice or clamp for holding down lead on a bench or table while it is pulled by hand from the other end.

LEADING: The technique of assembling a window or panel using lead cames to hold the glass together.

MATTING: A term for creating shading tones when painting on glass. Different implements are used to remove the initial application of paint, thereby creating a variety of effects and textures.

MOUTH-BLOWN GLASS: Made by blowing molten glass into a "muff" or cylindrical bubble. The ends are then cut leaving a cylinder shape. A cut is made on the side of the glass and placed back in the kiln and it will fold out into a piece of flat glass.

OPALESCENT GLASS: Opaque or non-transparent glass associated with "Tiffany" lampshades. Generally machine-made.

OXIDATION: A condition which will occur on lead and copper foil if they are exposed to the atmosphere for too long before soldering. A rub with wire wool or a wirebrush is used before soldering to remove.

PAINT: A black brown vitreous enamel used with specialized brushes for decorating glass which is then "fired" in a kiln and fuses the paint to the surface of the glass.

RESIST: An adhesive backed material such as vinyl that is used to "mask" or protect select areas of glass when sandblasting or etching.

ROLLED GLASS: Refers to machine-made flat glass which as its name implies is made by molten glass passing through two parallel rollers.

ROUNDELS: Hand-spun or machine pressed circles of glass with smooth finished edges. Available in various sizes and colors.

RUNNING PLIERS: Specialized pliers that can be used for breaking a straight score on long narrow strips of glass.

SANDBLASTING: A technique where sand projected by a compressor abrades the surface of the glass. Sandblasting can penetrate deeply and can "carve" the surface of thick glass.

SCORE: The fine fracture line created on the surface of glass with the wheel of a glass cutter.

SCORING: The process of applying pressure and moving the glass cutter over the surface of the glass to produce a light fracture.

SEMI-ANTIQUE GLASS: Machine-made flat glass with little movement but brilliant colors.

SILVER STAIN: Applied like glass paint, this substance contains silver nitrate which will color glass when fired. During firing the stain penetrates the glass. It produces shades of yellow through amber.

SOLDER: A mixture of tin and lead used to bond lead cames and copper foil together. 50:50 or 40:60 generally used.

SOLDERING: Melting solder with a soldering iron on to the joints of lead or the edges of copper foiled glass to bond the pieces together.

SOLDERING IRON: Tool used for melting solder.

TALLOW: Wax candle used to rub on the joints of lead before soldering.

TAPPING: A technique which assists the breaking of glass by using the ball end of a cutter. The glass is tapped from underneath.

TEMPLATE: Paper or cardboard shape used to mark out a pattern on the glass prior to scoring.

TINNING: Melting a flat coating of solder over copper foil.

TRACING: Painting outlines on glass with trace paint.

Useful Addresses

USA

HOLLANDER GLASS EAST INC, 140 58th Street, Brooklyn, NY 11220. Tel: 718 439 6111

ED HOY'S STAINED GLASS, 999 East Chicago Avenue, Naperville, Ill 60540.

STUDIO DESIGN, 1761 R 34 So., Wall, NJ 07727. Tel: 908 681 6003

UNITED KINGDOM

KANSA CRAFT, The Old Flour Mill, Wath Road, Elsecar, Barnsley, S Yorks S74 8HW. Tel: 01226 747424

LEAD & LIGHT, 35a Hartland Road, London NW1 4DB. Tel: 0171-485 0997

TEMPSFORD STAINED GLASS, The Old School, Tempsford, Sandy, Beds. Tel: 01767 640235

AUSTRALIA

AUSTRALIAN STAINED GLASS PTY LTD, 39 Pyrmont Street, Pyrmont, NSW 2009. Tel: 02 660 7424/7444

THE STAINED GLASS SHOPPE, 129 Boundary Road, Peakhurst NSW 2210. Tel: 02 533 4333

THE AUSGLASS ASSOCIATION, PO Box 8089 Hindley Street, Adelaide, South Australia 5000. Tel: 08 364 3170

FITZROY STAINED GLASS, 392 Queen's Parade, North Fitzroy, Victoria 3068. Tel: 03 482 3622

THE STAINED GLASS CENTRE, 221 Hale Street, Petrie Terrace, Queensland 4000. Tel: 07 369 0914

NEW ZEALAND

A TOUCH OF GLASS, 670 Mt Albert Road, Royal Oak, Auckland. Tel: 625 9466

A BECKETT GLASS, 4/38 Jutland Road, Takapuna, Auckland. Tel: 09 486 6836

CHEVALIER LEADLIGHT COMPANY, 130 Kitchener Road, Milford, Auckland. Tel: 09 489 5671

CLARE STAINED GLASS, 23 Jervois Road, Ponsonby, Auckland. Tel: 09 360 1997

GLASS EXPRESSIONS, 220 Arthur Street, Onchunga, Auckland. Tel: 09 636 9903

LEADLIGHT WORLD, 12 Beaconsfield Road, Grey Lynn, Auckland. Tel: 09 376 4793

Index